Master the Art
of
Parenting
Children
with
ADHD

51 Stress Free Strategies to Promote Emotional Regulation, Boost Social Skills, Advocate for School Success, and Enhance a Harmonious Home Environment

Shannon Snyder

If you would like to access FREE parenting charts and resources to implement strategies IMMEDIATELY click/scan here

http://bit.ly/3AvAkX0

This book is dedicated to my son, who has shown immense perseverance and strength. Despite the challenges and hardships brought on by ADHD, he has risen above them with courage and determination. His success is a testament to his unwavering spirit and resilience.
I dedicate this work to him, in admiration of his achievements and in celebration of the incredible person he has become. His story is an inspiration, not only to me but to everyone who faces their own challenges with gaining mastery over ADHD.

"To be proud of your children is one of the greatest joys a parent can experience."

— Anonymous

Contents

Introduction

"While we try to teach our children all about life, our children teach us what life is all about."

— *Angela Schwindt*

Every evening felt like a battleground. My six-year-old son sat at the kitchen table day after day, exhausted and crying in frustration. Pencils snapped, papers flew– tears from both of us were frequent visitors. Homework time, a simple daily routine for many, was, for us, a stark reminder of the unique challenges of parenting a child with ADHD. I did not realize this then, but immense potential and strength lay within these struggles. This book is born from those intense, heartwrenching moments and the transformative journey that followed.

This book is structured to help you understand ADHD, develop effective parenting strategies, enhance emotional and social skills, and navigate the educational system. It further explores lifestyle adjustments and nutritional tips that can make a real difference, all while providing the support you need as a caregiver. Unlike typical perspectives that view ADHD as a deficit, this book celebrates it as a distinct set of abilities, emphasizing the extraordinary potential for success and fulfillment inherent in these children. It recognizes ADHD as a different ability rather than a disability, infusing our approach with positivity and empowerment. This book will draw on diverse experiences from parents, educators, and experts. You are not alone in this journey. Together, we can shift the narrative around ADHD, focusing on strengths and possibilities.

What sets this guide apart is its blend of personal anecdotes, grounded in real-world experiences, with evidence-based strategies and practical advice you can immediately implement. This book isn't just a manual; it's a companion. As a mother of three, navigating ADHD became a significant part of my life when my son was diagnosed in second grade. The journey wasn't easy. Facing a school system ready to set limits on his potential, I took on the role of advocate, educator, and student. The lessons learned, and victories earned culminated into the creation of this book. Use this guide for your needs when you need it. Start by reading Chapter 1 completely; however, utilize the *Table of Contents* to your advantage afterward. This book is meant to meet you where you are in your journey. While all chapters will touch you in some way, some may be more important for you to read now. If you are worried your child is not getting the right services at school, jump to "Chapter 8: Ensuring Your Child Thrives in Educational Settings." If you are told your child is hitting other children, skip to "Chapter 3: Navigating Emotional Growth: The Parental Influence." If your child feels they may feel different than other children, read Chapter 1, "How to Explain ADHD to Your Child." Most importantly, if you start to feel overwhelmed and stressed, read Chapter 13, "Taking Care of Yourself While Caring for Your Child." This book may appear to have some areas of duplicate information, but that is purposeful since some strategies overlap a bit. For instance, Chapter 5, "Creating a Harmonious Environment," may note the same home environment strategy as Chapter 9, "Preparing for School Transitions" but each gives it's own further explanation for that topic of discussion. Remember, this book is for you to Master Parenting a Child with ADHD. It is a toolkit to get you where you want to be.

You bought this book because the ADHD journey is difficult. I hope to give you what I did not have. This guide meets you where you are in your journey, offering support and practical, actionable advice that can transform daily challenges into opportunities for growth and joy.

By the end of this book, you will have a toolkit that empowers you to approach ADHD with confidence, optimism, and a proactive mindset. It's about turning daily struggles into stepping stones for success and deepening your connection with your child. Let's step forward with an open heart and an eager mind, ready to embrace the challenges and joys of raising a child with ADHD.

Chapter 1
The ADHD Diagnosis Journey

"The genes of our ancestors lay the foundation, but it is the love and guidance of our parents that build the masterpiece."

— Unknown

When you first learn that your child has ADHD, it can bring a mix of feelings and questions. You might feel relieved to have a name for the struggles but also unsure about what to do next. Knowing that ADHD is most often a result of neurological issues can help you understand why your child acts the way they do. This knowledge can guide you in helping your child and advocating for them. It can also make you feel more confident in supporting your child. You might want to jump straight to the strategies for handling ADHD, and this chapter might seem complicated, but it's important to know there is a reason for your child's behavior. In the past, there was mainly one kind of medicine to treat ADHD, but now, with new research, there are many different ways to help kids and adults with ADHD based on their unique needs.

The Role of Genetics in ADHD: What Parents Need to Know

Heritability of ADHD

Current research robustly supports that ADHD is not merely a product of environmental influences or parenting styles but has strong genetic roots. Studies indicate that when a child is diagnosed with ADHD, there is about a 75% chance that genetics is a contributing factor. This high level of heritability places ADHD among the most inheritable psychological diagnoses, comparable to height in terms of genetic determination. Traits associated with ADHD are passed down through families, making it quite common to find multiple family members who may exhibit ADHD symptoms or have the diagnosis themselves. Understanding this can alleviate misplaced guilt or blame parents might feel about their child's behavior, redirecting energy toward management and support.

Genetic Testing and ADHD

While the idea of a genetic test that can conclusively diagnose ADHD is compelling, the reality is more complex. Currently, there is no single genetic test that can diagnose ADHD. However, ongoing advances in genetic research have identified genes that are specifically associated with an increased risk of ADHD.

- **SLC6A3 Gene:** Has been connected to those with the 5R/5R Genotype had a higher rate of being diagnosed with ADHD.
- **ADGRL3 Gene**: Research led by Dr. Matt Parker at the University of Surrey identified the ADGRL3 gene as closely linked to ADHD and shown to play a role in behaviors such as inattention and impulsivity. The study showed that issues within this gene were reversible with ADHD medication.
- **27 Genetic Variants:** An international study by Aarhus University identified 27 genetic variants (loci) associated with ADHD.

These findings are crucial for developing potential future treatments and may one day lead to more personalized approaches to managing the disorder. For now, genetic testing can inform if your child is at a higher risk of ADHD but should be a part of a broader diagnostic process that includes clinical evaluations and behavioral assessments.

Understanding Environmental Factors

While genetics play a pivotal role in ADHD, environmental factors also significantly impact the expression of symptoms. Factors have been linked to higher instances of ADHD, such as prenatal exposure to toxins, low birth weight, or premature birth. Additionally, overly chaotic environments, lack of structure, or inconsistency can exacerbate symptoms in children genetically predisposed to ADHD. This intertwining of genetic and environmental factors is crucial in understanding why each child's presentation of ADHD can be so unique and why tailored, individual approaches to treatment are necessary.

Neurodiversity and ADHD: A New Perspective

When my son was first diagnosed with ADHD, I felt like I was trying to understand a lot of complicated medical terms and many different behavior management ideas. It wasn't until I delved into the brain science of ADHD that I began to see my child not as a collection of symptoms but as a unique individual with a uniquely wired brain. Unfortunately for me, this understanding did not occur in his early years. I wish it had because this understanding transformed our approach to daily challenges and opened a pathway of empathy and effective intervention.

Neurodiversity

The word "neurodiversity" might be new, but it has important concepts, especially for people with ADHD. Neurodiversity means thinking about brain function differently: it sees people with ADHD, autism, and dyslexia as having different human brains. This idea challenges the old way of thinking that these differences are problems. Instead, it suggests that these differences are just different ways brains can work. The neurodiversity idea helps people by focusing on their strengths and encouraging society to make changes to support all kinds of brains, not just typical ones.

All of that jargon may be overwhelming, but what is important is how it affects your child. ADHD's placement within the neurodiversity movement is both a validation and a call to action. It aligns with a broader push for acceptance, understanding, and accommodation in schools, workplaces, and communities. This alignment helps dismantle the stigma often associated with ADHD by framing the condition as a part of the natural variety of human cognition rather than a disorder that needs to be cured. Schools that embrace this model can move towards more personalized learning approaches, appreciating that children with ADHD might need different kinds of support and can contribute uniquely to the classroom environment. This awareness can lead to more inclusive practices in the workplace that allow individuals with ADHD to employ their particular skills, such as creative problem-solving and the ability to think outside conventional frameworks.

However, thinking about neurodiversity doesn't mean ignoring the challenges people with ADHD face in a world mainly made for neurotypical people. These challenges can include dealing with schools that don't match your child's learning style or workplaces that misunderstand energy and creativity as not paying attention. Neurotypical people often miss the unique strengths people with ADHD have, which can lead to them being misunderstood. For example, their ability to focus intensely and develop ideas quickly can lead to great success in art, engineering, and starting new businesses. You must recognize and support these abilities and turn challenges into valuable strengths.

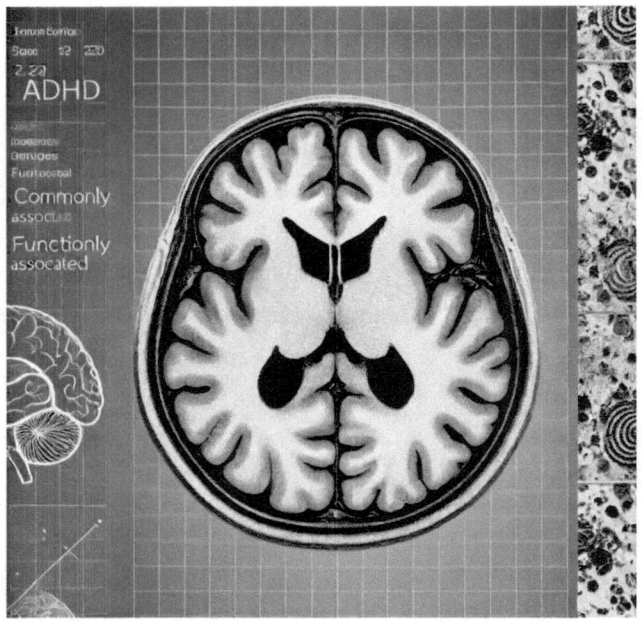

Advancements in brain imaging, such as MRI, have revealed structural differences in the brains of individuals with ADHD compared to those without the condition. These studies show variations in the size of specific brain regions and their activity levels, particularly areas that control attention and inhibitory control. Research by Dr. Amin and others in the field has illuminated how ADHD affects neural pathways, particularly those responsible for attention, impulsivity, and executive functioning. These areas, located primarily in the frontal cortex, are critical for high-level tasks such as planning, decision-making, and moderating social behavior. Such findings underscore ADHD as a neurological condition. Your child is not a result of poor parenting or how you do or do not discipline your child, as was commonly misconceived in earlier times.

Neurotransmitters in Action

Neurotransmitters, like dopamine and norepinephrine, are critical in the ADHD brain. These chemicals help send signals between brain cells and control mood, sleep, attention, and learning. In people with ADHD, an imbalance of these chemicals causes problems with signal transmission, leading to symptoms like not paying attention, being very active, and acting without thinking. ADHD treatments often focus on fixing these imbalances with medicine or therapy to help the brain manage these chemicals better.

Identifying ADHD: Signs, Symptoms, and Diagnosis

When you first think your child might have ADHD, the signs and symptoms can be confusing. It's important to know that these symptoms can appear differently. Some common signs are trouble focusing, while others, like mood swings, might be less obvious. Children with ADHD might have difficulty paying attention and staying focused on tasks or play or be very active and impulsive, like fidgeting or being unable to sit still. However, getting a professional evaluation is essential because these behaviors can also be expected for many children as they grow.

ADHD symptoms can be very different from one child to another, which is why it's called a spectrum. Some children might have mild symptoms that don't affect their daily lives, while others might have severe symptoms that make school and social interactions difficult. This difference can sometimes delay diagnosis, especially in mild cases where children learn to hide their difficulties. Some children might have trouble paying attention without being very active, which can be less noticeable to parents and teachers who expect to see hyperactivity.

Early Childhood Signs

In toddlers and preschoolers, ADHD symptoms often appear differently than in older children, making early detection a subtle but important process. Common indicators include an unusually high activity level beyond typical toddler energy. These little ones might frequently switch from one activity to another, unable to focus long enough, even on tasks or games they enjoy. They may struggle with sitting still during story time or resist activities that require quiet, focused engagement—like puzzle assembly or coloring. There are sometimes subtle hints, such as having play dates, seeing your child playing off to the side, and not engaging in group play. It's not just the physical restlessness but also the challenge of following simple instructions that might hint at ADHD. You might notice that your child doesn't listen like other kids. You may have to correct them for the same thing many times, which can feel very different from what other parents experience.

Early detection is crucial. It allows for interventions that can make starting school easier and reduce frustrations from untreated ADHD symptoms. Recognizing these early signs can lead to support that helps your child develop and helps you create routines that support their learning and growth.

ADHD in School-Aged Children

As children with ADHD enter school, their challenges often become more apparent—and sometimes more misunderstood. These children might struggle academically with staying organized, following detailed instructions, or completing homework assignments. Their backpacks may seem like caverns of chaos, with crumpled papers and forgotten assignments. You may find that you sent signed documents to be returned to the teacher, which will still be there weeks later, even though the teacher reminds the children to hand in their papers. Socially, the impulsivity of ADHD can make it hard for children to get along with their peers. They might interrupt others, intrude on games, or struggle to wait their turn, leading to conflicts or feeling left out. This behavior highlights the need for structured support at home and school. Interventions like IEPs (Individualized Education Programs) or 504 plans are essential for providing accommodations to create a learning environment that meets their needs. Strong collaboration between parents, teachers, and mental health professionals is critical to helping these children succeed academically and socially.

Adolescence and ADHD

Adolescence heralds a period of significant change where ADHD symptoms can evolve and sometimes intensify. The executive functioning challenges of ADHD can make the typical organizational demands of teenage life—such as managing schoolwork, extracurricular activities, and social life—overwhelming. Risk-taking behaviors may become more pronounced, driven by impulsivity and a desire for acceptance. Moreover, issues like low self-esteem, identity struggles, and anxiety about fitting in can be magnified. The social landscape becomes more complicated as friendships, and peer relationships involve more complex social cues and expectations. Emotional support and understanding from adults are crucial during this time. Strategies that help develop self-regulation and coping skills are vital, assisting teens to handle the challenges of adolescence with greater resilience.

ADHD in Adulthood

For adults, ADHD continues to influence professional paths and personal relationships significantly. Workplace challenges often include time management, meeting deadlines, and staying organized. Forgotten commitments or impulsive decisions can strain relationships. However, with awareness and appropriate strategies, adults with ADHD can thrive. Work environments with flexible schedules or tasks can be conducive, as can relationships built on understanding and open communication. Continual management strategies, such as therapy, coaching, or medication, remain important. Adults with ADHD often excel in careers that match their dynamic energy and creativity, turning potential challenges into strengths. Emphasizing problem-solving, resilience, and thinking outside the box can lead to fulfilling careers and relationships. Recognizing and adapting to ADHD at this stage can pave the way for success and satisfaction in various aspects of life.

Common Diagnosis Processes

Typically, the process of obtaining an ADHD diagnosis involves several steps. Initially, it often starts with a consultation with a pediatrician who can rule out other medical conditions that might mimic ADHD symptoms, such as hearing or vision problems. If ADHD is still suspected, the next step usually involves a detailed assessment carried out by a psychologist or psychiatrist specialized in child developmental disorders. This assessment may include interviews, standardized behavior rating scales, direct observation, and, in some cases, neuropsychological testing. These tools help to gather comprehensive information about the child's behavior across different settings and compare it to developmental norms. Here are the common elements you can expect to find in such a report:

1. Patient Information:
- Name, age, and other demographic details of the patient.
- Date of evaluation.

2. Referral Information:
- Reason for referral, such as difficulties in attention, hyperactivity, or impulse control.
- Source of referral (e.g., pediatrician, teacher, self, or family member).

3. Background Information:
- Developmental history including prenatal, perinatal, and early developmental milestones.
- Educational and occupational history.
- Medical history, including any previous diagnoses or treatments.
- Family history of ADHD or other psychiatric conditions.

4. Clinical Interview:
- Summary of the clinical interview with the patient and, if applicable, with family members or significant others.
- Observations about the patient's behavior and interactions during the evaluation.

5. Behavioral Observations:
- Description of the patient's behavior during the assessment, noting any signs of inattention, hyperactivity, or impulsivity.

6. Assessment Procedures and Results:
- A list of psychological tests and questionnaires were administered, such as the Conners scale, ADHD Rating Scale, or Continuous Performance Tests.

- Results and interpretation of these assessments highlighting areas that meet the diagnostic criteria for ADHD.

7. Diagnostic Impressions:
- Based on the DSM-5 or other relevant criteria, a detailed explanation of whether the patient meets the criteria for ADHD and the subtype (Predominantly Inattentive, Predominantly Hyperactive-Impulsive, or Combined).
- Discussion of any comorbid conditions identified during the assessment.

8. Recommendations:
- Specific treatment recommendations may include medication, psychotherapy, behavioral strategies, or accommodations at school or work.
- Suggestions for follow-up assessments or monitoring.

9. Summary and Conclusions:
- A concise summary of the findings and the rationale for the diagnosis.
- Final conclusions and any additional comments or considerations.

10. Appendices (if applicable):
- Copies of questionnaires or detailed scores of tests.
- Additional notes or records used during the assessment.

This report is used by healthcare providers to thoroughly understand the patient's condition and plan appropriate treatment and interventions. It also serves as formal documentation that can be used in educational or occupational settings to arrange necessary accommodations.

Interpreting the results of these assessments is a delicate process that requires professional expertise. Parents must understand that these results provide insights into their child's unique behavioral patterns and cognitive strengths and weaknesses. The assessment results can pinpoint specific challenges in executive functioning, attention, or impulse control, which are critical for developing targeted interventions. Moreover, understanding these results can empower you as a parent. It enables you to advocate effectively for your child in educational settings and helps you choose appropriate strategies and supports that align with their needs.

Navigating an ADHD diagnosis requires patience and persistence. It involves collecting a lot of information to ensure the diagnosis is correct and the right treatments are chosen. By understanding ADHD and its different signs, you can become a knowledgeable advocate for your child, helping them manage the condition and improve their quality of life. But you are not alone. The professionals and school personnel you involve will help guide you through the process and empower you to be there for your child.

Comorbidity

Comorbid conditions are frequently present alongside ADHD, which can complicate diagnosis and treatment. It is not uncommon for children with ADHD to also experience learning disabilities, anxiety disorders, or mood disorders. These conditions can intersect, making identifying all the underlying issues challenging without a thorough evaluation. For example, a child struggling with both ADHD and dyslexia may become highly frustrated with schoolwork, leading to behavioral problems that might initially be attributed solely to ADHD. Understanding these overlaps is crucial for developing an effective treatment plan that addresses all facets of a child's needs.

Common Learning Disabilities

Individuals with ADHD (Attention-Deficit/Hyperactivity Disorder) often experience co-occurring learning disabilities. These can affect their academic performance, organizational skills, and ability to process information. Here are some of the learning disabilities commonly associated with ADHD:

Dyslexia:
- Definition: Dyslexia is a learning disorder that makes it hard to recognize words accurately or fluently and causes problems with spelling and decoding. These difficulties usually come from a problem with the phonological part of language, which is surprising because other cognitive skills are often unaffected.
- Impact on Learning: Individuals with dyslexia may struggle with reading comprehension, spelling, writing, and sometimes speech. They might read below the expected level for their age, need help processing verbal instructions, or take longer to perform reading or writing tasks.

Dyscalculia:
- Definition: Dyscalculia is a specific learning disorder involving difficulty learning or comprehending arithmetic. It includes problems with understanding numbers, manipulating numbers, performing mathematical calculations, and learning facts about mathematics.
- Impact on Learning: People with dyscalculia may struggle with basic arithmetic, have a poor understanding of math symbols, experience difficulties with time, measurement, and estimation, and often require alternative learning strategies for math.

Dysgraphia:
- Definition: Dysgraphia is a learning disability that affects writing. It makes it hard to remember and master the motor movements needed to write letters or numbers. Dysgraphia is characterized by difficulties with spelling, poor handwriting, and trouble putting thoughts on paper.
- Impact on Learning: This can manifest as poor handwriting, trouble with written expression (such as organizing ideas and using proper syntax), and difficulties with fine motor skills.

Executive Functioning Issues:
- Definition: Although not a specific learning disability, many individuals with ADHD have trouble with executive function. This term refers to the cognitive processes that manage other mental tasks, such as working memory, reasoning, task flexibility, problem-solving, planning, and execution.
- Impact on Learning: Challenges in executive function can lead to difficulties in organizing tasks, managing time, making decisions, and maintaining attention on schoolwork or projects.

Language Processing Disorder:
- Definition: A type of learning disability that affects an individual's understanding of spoken and written language. This can be a broader disorder encompassing receptive language (difficulty understanding language) and expressive language (difficulty using language to express oneself).
- Impact on Learning: Individuals may have difficulty understanding spoken language, following directions, and expressing thoughts verbally. This can lead to challenges in learning in traditional classroom settings that rely heavily on verbal instructions.

These learning disabilities often require tailored educational strategies and interventions. Recognizing and diagnosing these issues alongside ADHD is crucial for effective management and support.

Given the broad spectrum of how ADHD can present and the common occurrence of comorbid conditions, personalized treatment and support plans are essential. No single approach works for every child with ADHD; what may be effective for one child might not be suitable for another. Tailored interventions are necessary when meeting the needs of each unique child and may involve a combination of behavioral therapy, educational accommodations, medication, and family support. The goal is always to enhance the child's ability to function successfully across various settings, including home, school, and social environments.

After Diagnosis: The Emotions Behind an ADHD Diagnosis

When the reality of an ADHD diagnosis settles in, it ushers in a wave of emotions, not just for the child but for the entire family. The initial feelings can range from relief at having an explanation for previous challenges to anxiety about what the future holds. It's a period marked by an emotional rollercoaster, where days of optimism are interspersed with moments of overwhelming concern. For many parents, there is also the struggle of reconciling the child they know with the label introduced into their lives. Understanding and navigating this emotional landscape is crucial in moving forward constructively.

The Stages of Acceptance

The stages of acceptance after an ADHD diagnosis can often mirror those traditionally associated with grief: denial, anger, bargaining, depression, and acceptance. Initially, you might question the diagnosis, unwilling to align your vibrant, energetic child with the challenges the label suggests. This denial can shift into frustration or anger—why your child, why your family? It's a normal reaction from a deep-seated desire to protect your child from hardship. Bargaining may follow, with thoughts of what you could have done differently or how you might still find a way to mitigate the diagnosis. Depression or profound sadness can ensue as the permanence of the situation sinks in, accompanied by worries about your child's ability to navigate life with ADHD.

Moving through these stages isn't linear and doesn't occur on a set timeline. Each family, each parent, and each child will experience these emotions differently and on their own schedule. What's important is creating a supportive environment where these feelings can be expressed and addressed openly. Discussions validating your and your child's feelings about the diagnosis are essential. It helps in processing the emotional aspects of the diagnosis, ensuring that neither of you feels isolated in your experiences.

Channeling Your Emotions

For many parents, navigating the aftermath of an ADHD diagnosis is filled with concerns and questions. Will my child be able to succeed in school? How will this affect their social relationships? What does this mean for their future? Such questions are not only common but entirely expected. Addressing them involves a combination of education, support, and advocacy. Learning as much as you can about ADHD is a crucial first step. It equips you with the knowledge to make informed decisions about treatment options, educational strategies, and behavioral management techniques. Support groups, either in person or online, can be invaluable, providing a platform to gain strategies and share experiences with other parents facing similar challenges. These groups can also be a source of emotional support, helping to alleviate loneliness and misunderstanding by connecting you with others who truly 'get it.'

National Organizations for ADHD

Several national organizations offer support, resources, and information for individuals with ADHD and their families. Here are a few prominent ones:

CHADD (Children and Adults with Attention-Deficit/Hyperactivity Disorder)
• Website: www.chadd.org
• Description: CHADD is one of the most prominent advocacy groups in the United States dedicated to helping people affected by ADHD. They offer many resources, including support groups, educational programs, and up-to-date research and treatment options. They also provide a tool to search for local chapters and support groups.

ADDA (Attention Deficit Disorder Association)
• Website: www.add.org
• Description: ADDA specializes in the needs of adults with ADHD. The organization provides information, resources, and networking opportunities to help adults with ADHD lead better lives. Their services include webinars, virtual support groups, and conferences.

Understood.org
• Website: www.understood.org
• Description: Although not solely focused on ADHD, Understood.org provides broad support for individuals with learning and attention issues, including ADHD. The site offers

practical advice, step-by-step guides, interactive tools, and supportive community.

The National Resource Center on ADHD
• Website: www.help4adhd.org
• Description: A partnership between CHADD and the CDC, the National Resource Center on ADHD provides comprehensive information about ADHD to parents, educators, adults, and professionals. The website includes articles on symptoms, treatments, and strategies for managing ADHD.

These websites are valuable resources for anyone seeking support or more information about living with ADHD or helping someone who has the condition. They offer tools for connecting with others facing similar challenges, which can be incredibly supportive and helpful.

Post-Diagnosis

Treatment and Management Strategies

Post-diagnosis, the focus often shifts to treatment and management strategies. This phase should explore up-to-date treatment options, including medication, behavioral therapy, lifestyle changes, and educational interventions. This book examines each of these areas. Each child's needs will vary, and what works for one child might not work for another This personalized approach can feel daunting due to its trial-and-error nature. Still, it's also a process that can lead to discovering the most effective strategies to support your child's growth and development. Educational accommodations are also a critical area to explore. Understanding your child's legal rights to an appropriate education under laws such as the Individuals with Disabilities Education Act (IDEA) in the U.S. can empower you to advocate for necessary services and support in their educational setting. Chapters eight, nine, and ten guide you on how best to advocate for and obtain proper services for your child.

Navigating life after an ADHD diagnosis is a complex, ongoing process that involves much more than medical treatment. It's about understanding your child's world from their perspective, advocating for their needs, and educating those around them to foster a supportive network. It's also about recognizing and celebrating the strengths and unique talents that your child brings to the world. With the proper support and strategies, children with ADHD can and do thrive, leading rich, fulfilling lives marked by incredible creativity, resilience, and strength. As you move forward, remember that you are not alone. A whole community of parents, educators, and professionals is available to support you and your child every step of the way.

How to Explain ADHD to Your Child

Age-Appropriate Explanations

When the time comes to discuss ADHD with your child, the way you frame this conversation can significantly influence their self-perception and confidence. It's crucial to tailor your explanation to be age-appropriate, ensuring it is understandable and relatable. For younger children, simplifying the explanation by explaining how their brain works a little differently than their friends, and sometimes, it can be harder for them to sit still, pay attention, or remember things. It's like having a race car brain with bicycle brakes! Everyone's brain is unique, and there are particular things you can do to help them feel better and do their best.

For adolescents, you can explain that certain parts of their brain work differently, making it harder for them to focus, stay organized, or control impulses. ADHD is very common, and it's not their fault. It's just how their brain is wired. There are lots of strategies, tools, and sometimes medications that can help them manage ADHD. These can help them succeed in school, at home, and with friends. Understanding ADHD better can help you find the best ways to support them and use their unique strengths.

Focusing on Strengths

Central to your discussion should be a strong emphasis on the strengths and abilities that come with ADHD. Highlighting attributes such as creativity, enthusiasm, and the ability to think outside the box shifts the focus from deficits to capabilities. For instance, let your child know that many inventors and artists who likely had ADHD used their unique way of thinking to solve problems and create beautiful works. Refer to Chapter 14 for the names of famous individuals who had ADHD. You and your child will be pleasantly surprised. This approach helps children feel empowered, viewing ADHD not as a barrier but as a differentiator that can lead to success.

Using Stories and Resources

Introducing books and resources that portray ADHD positively can be remarkably effective. For younger children, books like "Eddie Enough!" by Debbie Zimmett provide relatable stories reflecting their experiences. Eddie Minetti is a third-grader who often gets into trouble at school due to his undiagnosed ADHD. The story follows Eddie as he struggles with his behavior, earning the nickname "Eddie Enough" from his classmates and teacher. The book highlights Eddie's challenges and the eventual diagnosis and treatment of his ADHD, which helps him manage his behavior better. For older children, "Percy Jackson" by Rick Riordan is about a 12-year-old boy named Percy Jackson who has both ADHD and dyslexia. He discovers he is a demigod and prevents the Titans from overthrowing the Olympian gods and destroying the world. These stories offer comfort and role models, showing that success is achievable.

Misdiagnoses and ADHD: Avoiding the Pitfalls

Finding the proper ADHD diagnosis can be challenging because other conditions can look like ADHD. Things like anxiety, depression, and sleep problems often have similar symptoms. For example, a child with anxiety might seem distracted or not paying attention, just like ADHD. Depression can also cause trouble concentrating and making decisions, making it hard to tell apart from ADHD. Sleep problems can make someone act and focus differently during the day, which can also look like ADHD. Because of these similarities, it's essential to have a careful and detailed evaluation to get the correct diagnosis.

Getting It Right the First Time

The importance of a comprehensive evaluation cannot be overstated. A thorough assessment for ADHD should encompass a variety of components, including a detailed medical history, behavioral assessments, interviews with parents and teachers, and possibly neuropsychological testing. This extensive approach is crucial because it helps to rule out other conditions that might be causing symptoms similar to those associated with ADHD. For example, hearing and vision tests are often recommended to exclude sensory deficits that might be mistaken for inattention. A thorough evaluation ensures that all possible underlying causes are considered before arriving at a diagnosis, thereby increasing the accuracy of the diagnosis and the effectiveness of subsequent treatment plans.

Misdiagnosis can lead to several significant challenges. If a child is incorrectly diagnosed with ADHD, they may be prescribed medication or therapies that are not only unhelpful but could potentially exacerbate their actual underlying condition. For instance, stimulant medications commonly used to treat ADHD could increase anxiety in a child whose inattentiveness is actually due to an anxiety disorder, not ADHD. Furthermore, an incorrect diagnosis can lead to critical delays in receiving the appropriate treatment for their actual condition, potentially impacting the child's academic performance, social development, and emotional well-being. The implications of a misdiagnosis extend beyond just the immediate treatment concerns; they can affect a child's self-esteem and self-understanding as they struggle with symptoms that are misidentified and, therefore, ineffectively managed.

Second Opinions

Given these risks, seeking a second opinion or consulting specialists is often advisable, particularly in complex cases where an initial evaluation does not lead to a precise diagnosis. Specialists in child psychology or psychiatry who have more profound expertise in ADHD and related disorders might offer more nuanced insights that can lead to a more accurate diagnosis. Additionally, they can employ specialized diagnostic tools and assessments that provide a broader view of the child's cognitive and behavioral profile. Consulting with a specialist can also help confirm the initial diagnosis, provide peace of mind, and ensure that the treatment plan is appropriate and targeted to the child's specific needs.

Debunking ADHD Myths: Separating Fact from Fiction

It Is Not Because of You

The landscape of ADHD is often shrouded in myths and misconceptions that can obscure the truth, leading to stigma and misjudgment. As someone who has navigated the complexities of ADHD within my own family, I understand the critical need to separate fact from fiction. One of the most pervasive myths is that ADHD is the result of poor parenting or a lack of discipline. This misconception can be particularly damaging as it places undue blame on parents, often making them feel inadequate or guilty for their child's behavior. ADHD is not a condition born from parenting styles but is a neurological disorder that is primarily influenced by genetics and brain chemistry. Children with ADHD do not lack discipline; instead, they face real challenges with executive function, which can affect their ability to organize, prioritize, and regulate their emotions and behavior.

Not All ADHD Is the Same

Another common misunderstanding is that ADHD is synonymous with hyperactivity. While hyperactivity is a well-known aspect of ADHD, it's crucial to recognize the breadth of the spectrum. ADHD manifests in three primary presentations: primarily hyperactive-impulsive, primarily inattentive, and combined. The predominantly inattentive presentation, previously known as ADD, involves symptoms like daydreaming, distractibility, and difficulty following instructions. This type often goes unnoticed because it lacks the overt hyperactivity associated with the disorder. Children and adults with this type of ADHD may be wrongly perceived as lazy or uninterested when, in fact, they are internally struggling to maintain focus and process information as efficiently as their peers.

The Gender Effect

Gender plays a significant role in how ADHD is perceived and diagnosed. Historically, ADHD has been underdiagnosed in females. This is partly because girls often exhibit the predominantly inattentive form of ADHD, which, as noted, can be less conspicuous than the hyperactive type. Additionally, societal expectations can influence the interpretation of symptoms. Hyperactivity in boys may be viewed as 'boys being boys,' whereas similar behavior might be seen as problematic in girls. Girls are often taught to be quieter and reserved; thus, their symptoms might manifest as daydreaming or being withdrawn and easily mistaken for shyness or introversion. The failure to recognize ADHD in girls can lead to years of struggles with self-esteem and academic challenges, compounded by the lack of appropriate interventions.

Intelligence

The myth that ADHD is linked to lower intelligence is false. ADHD affects attention and executive functioning but does not determine how smart someone is. People with ADHD have a wide range of intellectual abilities, and many excel in creative and academic fields. The challenge is not a lack of intelligence but finding ways to use their abilities in traditional learning or work environments. This false belief that ADHD means low IQ can be harmful and discouraging, hiding the strengths and potential of those with the disorder. With the right strategies and support, individuals with ADHD can achieve great things, often thinking creatively and being natural innovators.

By confronting these myths directly, we empower individuals with ADHD, their families, and educators. This approach enriches our understanding and helps create environments where each child can thrive according to their unique needs. Clarifying these misconceptions improves support systems and reduces the stigma that many children and adults with ADHD face daily. As we educate ourselves and others, we break down the barriers created by misinformation and start a more compassionate and informed discussion about what ADHD truly is.

Chapter 2
Helping Your Child Navigate Emotions and Relationships

"Emotions are a natural part of being human. Learning to navigate them is a lifelong journey that starts in childhood."

— *Unknown*

I magine the world through the eyes of your child with ADHD: a place where sights and sounds rush in like a wave, feelings can be overwhelming like a storm, and each day brings new challenges in managing a whirlwind of emotions. As a parent, your role in guiding your child through this emotional landscape is vital and profound. This chapter is dedicated to helping you understand and develop tools to help your child navigate their emotions effectively, which are essential for their growth and well-being.

Emotional Regulation: Tools and Techniques for Children

Emotional regulation is a complex skill, even more so for children with ADHD, who often experience emotions more intensely. You must first help your child manage their feelings by understanding what triggers them. Triggers can vary widely; they might include a change in routine, sensory overload, or even feelings of frustration from struggling with tasks that their peers accomplish easily. Observing your child closely and noting what precipitates emotional outbursts can provide invaluable insights. You might start by journaling incidents that led to outbursts, noting what happened just before the incident, the environment, and other potential external triggers. Completing this journal might reveal patterns, such as specific times of day, certain interactions, or activities that consistently lead to frustration or anger. For example, completing homework in the late afternoon might frequently trigger outbursts, possibly due to accumulated stress from the school day or fatigue. Once you identify these triggers, , teaching your child coping strategies can help manage their reactions.

Sample Trigger Journal

Date	
What happened just before the incident?	
Describe the activity or interaction that preceded the incident.	
Note any specific comments or actions that might have triggered the reaction.	
Detail the emotional or behavioral reactions, including any physical reactions (crying, laughing, yelling).	
Specify where the incident occurred (classroom, playground, dining room).	
Describe the environmental conditions (noisy, hot, dimly lit, crowded).	
List the individuals present (teacher, sibling, peers).	
Identify any sensory triggers (loud sounds, bright lights).	
Describe any interactions with others that might have influenced the reaction (peer conflict, adult directives).	
Note any recent changes in routine or known stressors that might affect behavior.	
Any other observations or relevant information.	
Describe how the situation was handled immediately after the incident.	

Getting Your Child to Recognize Their Own Emotions

Once you've identified potential triggers, the next foundational step is helping your child recognize and label their emotions. This is crucial, as many children with ADHD react impulsively to their feelings because they cannot identify them in time to manage them effectively. Introducing tools like emotion charts or mood thermometers can be incredibly beneficial here. These visual aids serve as external representations of what they feel inside, helping children with ADHD articulate their emotions before they become overwhelming. For instance, using a mood thermometer, children can gauge their feelings on a scale from cool (calm) to hot (angry), which helps them communicate their state of mind to you and other caregivers effectively.

ANGRY
I feel mad! I need to calm down or I will say something or do something I should not do.

FRUSTRATED
I feel stressed! I need to take a break so I do not get into trouble.

WORRIED
I need help because I can't stop thinking about something that is bothering me.

SAD
I'm not feeling good, I want to cry and need help.

CALM
I am calm. Nothing is bothering me and I am enjoying everything around me.

HAPPY
I am happy! I am smiling or laughing.

An emotional chart for kids, often called a "feelings chart" or "mood chart," is a visual tool designed to help children identify and express their emotions. These charts are handy for younger children who may not have the vocabulary to express their feelings or those who struggle with emotional regulation.

I feel:

Emotional charts can be used at home, in classrooms, or in therapeutic settings to support children's emotional learning and communication. They are simple yet effective tools for aiding children's emotional development. I created an emotional regulation coloring book on Amazon that is available to help children identify their emotions and give them time to calm down by coloring. There are two different versions based on age.

The Complete Guide to Support Children by Navigating Emotions to Promote Healthy Relationships and Self-Control

EMOTIONAL REGULATION COLORING BOOK FOR KIDS AGES 3-8

by Shannon Snyder

Bonus Step-By Step Instructions for Caretakers

Ideal for Neurodevelopmental Disorders, Trauma, Anxiety, Behavioral Issues, and Learning Disabilities.

EMOTIONAL REGULATION COLORING BOOK FOR KIDS AGES 8-12

The Guide to Help Children Navigate Their Emotions Resulting in Self-Control and Healthy Relationships

Bonus Instructions for Caretakers

Empathy plays a pivotal role in this process. Responding to your child's emotional outbursts with compassion and understanding, rather than punishment or frustration, is critical. It's about validating their feelings, letting them know it's okay to feel upset or angry, and guiding them toward appropriate expressions. This empathetic approach calms the immediate situation and models how to handle their emotions constructively for your child.

To equip your child with self-regulating methods, introduce simple, child-friendly techniques to calm the body and mind. Deep breathing exercises are practical and can be taught and practiced anywhere, anytime. Have your child breathe in slowly through their nose, hold for a count of three and exhale slowly through their mouth. This kind of breathing helps reduce the physiological symptoms of stress and can quickly help bring emotions back into balance.

Progressive muscle relaxation is another technique that can be particularly helpful for children who experience physical tension with emotional stress. This technique involves tightening and then relaxing different muscle groups in the body. It can be turned into a fun routine by pretending to squish and then releasing a giant imaginary lemon with each hand!

One effective and research-based breathing technique for children is guided deep breathing using a simple animated video, as demonstrated in a study by Stanford researchers. This study found that children can significantly reduce their physiological arousal—measured by changes in heart rate and respiratory sinus arrhythmia—by following a one-minute video instructing them to take slow, deep breaths. The video guides children to inhale as if smelling a flower and exhale as if blowing out a candle, making it engaging and easy to follow. This practical approach has been tested in everyday settings like playgrounds and day camps, showing real-life applicability.

Role-Playing Scenarios

Role-playing scenarios are a dynamic way to help your child prepare for emotional situations they find challenging. By re-enacting various scenarios, such as dealing with a change in plans or reacting to bullying from a peer, you provide your child with a safe space to practice their responses. Through these rehearsals, your child can learn to pause before reacting, consider their feelings, and choose a more thoughtful action.

Discussion After Role-Play:
• Ask the child how they felt during the role-play.
• Discuss what went well and what could be improved.
• Talk about other ways to handle the situation.
• Emphasize the importance of talking to a teacher or a trusted adult if the teasing continues or they feel unsafe.

Tips for Effective Role-Playing:
• Validate Feelings: Let the child know that it's okay to feel upset about being teased and that they have the right to ask others to stop.
• Practice Different Outcomes: Role-play the same scenario multiple times, with different responses from the "peers" to help the child adapt to various reactions.
• Focus on Confidence: Encourage the child to use a strong, confident voice and maintain eye contact, which can help them assert themselves.

In conclusion, managing emotions is a critical skill for all children, especially those with ADHD. By understanding emotional triggers, teaching your child to recognize and label their feelings, responding with empathy, and equipping them with practical relaxation techniques, you empower them to navigate their emotional world more effectively. These strategies enhance their emotional intelligence and improve their relationships and overall quality of life, laying a foundation for long-term resilience and success.

Techniques for Managing Anger and Frustration

Identifying Triggers

Emotions such as anger and frustration can frequently surface in the life of a child with ADHD, often with an intensity that surprises both the child and those around them. Understanding how to navigate these strong emotions is crucial for the child's development and the overall harmony of your home. As with all emotional regulation, the first step in this process involves identifying specific triggers that precipitate these feelings of anger and frustration. Once these triggers are better understood, teaching your child coping strategies can significantly help manage their reactions. Validate their emotions by acknowledging their feelings. For example, "I see you're upset. Let's talk about it." Set boundaries of acceptable behavior and the consequences of losing their temper. Praise and reward the child when they handle their anger well. Positive reinforcement can encourage them to use coping strategies.

Encourage them to take deep breaths to calm down. You can practice this together: inhale deeply through the nose, hold, and exhale slowly through the mouth. Encourage them to use "I" statements to express their feelings. For example, "I feel mad when…" Create a quiet space where the child can go to calm down when they're feeling angry. Fill it with calming activities or items. Physical activity plays a pivotal role in managing ADHD symptoms, particularly emotional regulation. Encourage them to go outside and shoot basketball, jump on a trampoline, or go for a run. These basic techniques are incorporated with your emotional regulation, which is our next topic.

Modeling Behavior

How you respond to your child's expressions of anger and frustration sets a cornerstone for how they manage these emotions independently. Displaying calmness and patience in the face of your child's anger not only models those traits but also helps to de-escalate the situation. When a child is met with yelling or punishment, it can often exacerbate their feelings and lead to heightened distress. Instead, try to maintain a composed demeanor and use a gentle tone to express their feelings. Validate their emotions by acknowledging their feelings and expressing understanding. For instance, saying, "I see that you are upset right now, and that's okay. Let's try some deep breaths together," can be more effective than demands for immediate calmness. This approach soothes the present moment and strengthens your child's trust in you as a source of support, not fear, during challenging times. I was a 911 dispatcher, and when people are in crisis, they are not calm. One successful technique in every situation was maintaining a quiet voice despite their yelling. If I would have raised my voice, that would have escalated them. I would ask the question over and over again in the same calm tone until they calmed down enough to give me the information. Giving validity to their excitement or feelings of fear was imperative, but always speaking in the same tone was the key. This technique worked very well in my family life. Don't get me wrong, I could not always use this technique, but things worked out much better when I did. Remember, each child is unique, and you might need to adjust these strategies and be patient to find what works best for your child's needs and personality.

Understanding Sensory Processing in ADHD

Sensory processing is a term that frequently surfaces in conversations about ADHD, yet its complexities are often not fully understood. Essentially, sensory processing refers to how our nervous system interprets and responds to sensory information from the environment—everything from the texture of our clothes to the sound of a car horn. For children with ADHD, this process can often be overwhelming, as their nervous systems may hyper-respond or under-respond to sensory stimuli, making what might be a minor annoyance to some feel intolerable to them. This heightened sensitivity can significantly impact their emotional regulation, leading to distress and even behavioral outbursts when sensory information becomes too much to handle comfortably.

Identifying Sensory Sensitivities

Identifying sensory sensitivities in children with ADHD involves keen observation and sometimes even a bit of detective work. Signs that a child may struggle with sensory processing issues include overreacting to physical contact, complaints about clothing being itchy or uncomfortable, distress in loud environments, or an unusual need for movement. These sensitivities can directly impact a child's ability to focus, stay calm, or feel comfortable in typical settings like a classroom or a family dinner at a restaurant. Recognizing these signs early can help you intervene to mitigate discomfort and support better overall emotional regulation.

Creating Sensory-Friendly Environments

Creating a sensory-friendly environment is a proactive step in supporting a child with ADHD. This means designing a personal space at home that minimizes sensory overload. Use calming colors for room decor, invest in comfortable clothing and bedding, and consider the home's acoustics—softening harsh sounds with carpets or curtains can make a significant difference. Lighting also plays a crucial role; natural light is ideal, but soft, non-flickering artificial lights are preferred if they are not possible. In school settings, advocating for accommodations like noise-canceling headphones during high-noise periods or permission to use fidget tools can help your child manage sensory input and maintain focus and calm.

Incorporating Sensory-Integration Activities

Incorporating sensory integration activities into your child's routine can also be beneficial. These activities are designed to help children adapt to sensory input more effectively, making them less likely to become overwhelmed. Occupational therapy, often recommended for children with sensory processing challenges, uses techniques tailored to each child's needs. These might include therapeutic brushing, joint compressions, or customized exercise routines that help desensitize the nervous system to sensory stimuli. Therapeutic brushing, also known as the Wilbarger Protocol, is a technique that involves using a surgical brush to provide deep-pressure touch stimulation to the skin. This method is believed to help desensitize the nervous system to sensory input, which can reduce symptoms of sensory overload. Joint compressions typically follow the brushing and should be performed under the guidance of a trained professional to ensure safety and effectiveness. Joint compressions involve applying gentle pressure to the joints, which can provide stimulus input that helps calm the nervous system. The pressure is applied systematically to joints to help increase body awareness and decrease overall sensory sensitivity. It's typically used to help manage reactions to sensory input and improve focus and attention. Customized exercise routines tailored to an individual's sensory needs can also help desensitize the nervous system. These routines might include activities that provide:

- Vestibular stimulation (like swinging or spinning)
- Proprioceptive input (like jumping or pushing heavy objects)
- Tactile stimulation (like playing with textured toys)

These exercises aim to engage the sensory system in a controlled manner, gradually increasing tolerance to various stimuli. These techniques are usually part of a broader therapeutic approach and should be administered by professionals trained in sensory integration therapy. At home, simple activities like playing with playdough, sand, or water can also serve as sensory play that helps children learn to process sensory inputs more effectively.

Teaching Self-Advocacy

Teaching self-advocacy is an empowering tool for children with ADHD and sensory processing issues. It involves helping your child recognize the signs that sensory overload is imminent and equipping them with the language and confidence to express their needs. For example, they might learn to say, "I'm feeling overwhelmed right now; can we leave this noisy place?" or "The lights here are too bright for me; can we dim them?" By supporting your child to advocate for their needs, you empower them to manage their sensory challenges proactively and confidently, ensuring they have the tools to seek comfort in environments that might otherwise feel overwhelming. This skill not only aids in immediate sensory regulation but also builds a foundation for self-awareness and advocacy that will serve them throughout life, fostering independence and resilience.

The Emotional Landscape of a Child with ADHD

Children with ADHD often navigate a world where their emotional responses are more intense and less predictable than those of their peers. This heightened emotional sensitivity means that feelings of joy, frustration, or sadness are not just mere reactions but can feel all-consuming and overwhelming. A minor setback can evoke a disproportionate response for these children, and positive events can lead to unusually high excitement. Understanding this aspect of ADHD can profoundly affect how you, as a parent, respond to and support these children in their emotional development.

Rejection Sensitive Dysphoria (RSD)

One particularly challenging aspect of this emotional sensitivity is known as Rejection Sensitive Dysphoria (RSD). RSD is prevalent among individuals with ADHD and involves an intense emotional response to the perception of rejection or failure. Children with RSD may experience sudden feelings of sadness, anger, or anxiety when they perceive that they are criticized or rejected, even if this perception is not aligned with the intentions or actions of others. The pain felt from these perceived rejections can be profound and debilitating, causing the child to withdraw from situations where they fear rejection might occur again. These behaviors can be a reluctance to try new activities or becoming extremely upset over seemingly minor corrections. Understanding RSD is the first step in helping these children navigate their complex emotional responses.

Strategies for Rejection Sensitive Dysphoria

When it comes to strategies for RSD, evidence-based approaches can offer significant benefits. One effective strategy is the IDEAL model, which involves structured problem-solving by helping children identify the problem, develop potential solutions, weigh the pros and cons of each, and decide on the best course of action. This method helps manage immediate emotional distress and teaches valuable skills for handling future challenges. Another method is Stop-Think-Plan-Do-Review. This method involves stopping and calming down, thinking about the problem and possible solutions, planning the best solution and action, and reviewing the outcome.

Additionally, teach assertive communication skills to express feelings and needs without aggression or passivity. Encourage your child to consider other people's perspectives to reduce misinterpretations of social interactions. Provide strategies for resolving conflicts positively and constructively. Encourage them to treat themselves with the kindness they would offer a friend. Help them understand that everyone experiences rejection and failure and they are not alone. Teach them to observe their emotions without judgment.

Finally, cognitive-behavioral techniques can be adapted for children, allowing them to identify and challenge the often negative thought patterns that can accompany ADHD and RSD. For example, teaching a child to recognize thoughts like "Nobody likes me" as distortions of reality and to reframe them into more accurate and less distressing thoughts can significantly alleviate emotional distress.

Incorporating Support Systems

The role of support systems in managing the emotional landscape of children with ADHD cannot be overstressed. A supportive environment at home and school is a crucial buffer against the stressors these children face. At home, this means creating an atmosphere where feelings are openly discussed and validated, where the child feels secure in expressing their emotions without fear of judgment or ridicule. In educational settings, support might look like teachers who are aware of and sensitive to the emotional triggers of their students with ADHD and who are equipped with strategies to help these students navigate their feelings. Moreover, peer support plays an integral role; facilitating positive peer interactions and friendships can provide children with ADHD with essential emotional support and a sense of belonging.

As we wrap up this chapter, it's clear that helping a child with ADHD navigate their emotions requires patience, understanding, and proactive strategies. By recognizing their heightened emotional sensitivity, addressing Rejection Sensitive Dysphoria (RSD), implementing structured emotional regulation techniques, and fostering supportive environments, we aim to equip children with the tools they need to manage and express their emotions healthily and constructively.

As you've been navigating through the insights and strategies shared in this book, I hope you've found value in the preceding pages that unfold the complexities and the potential of raising a successful child. The subsequent chapters contain additional information and strategies to help you. I have aimed to provide you with knowledge and tools that enlighten and empower you and your family. I would be deeply grateful if you could share your thoughts through a review. Your review could be the very thing that encourages another parent to pick up this book and find the support and understanding they need to make their journey a little easier, a little less lonely.

https://amzn.to/3XeYwEO

Let's continue your journey to success and healing!

Chapter 3
Navigating Emotional Growth: The Parental Influence

"The way we talk to our children becomes their inner voice."

— *Peggy O'Mara*

For any parent, watching your child struggle with intense emotions can create a strong desire to help them find peace and balance. This feeling is even more vital for parents of children with ADHD, as emotional dysregulation often comes with inattention, hyperactivity, and impulsivity. It's not just about managing these symptoms—it's about understanding the emotions behind them and guiding your child toward emotional maturity. This chapter explores the power of empathy in parenting. Empathy deepens your connection with your child and helps them navigate their emotions with greater awareness and skill.

Parenting with Empathy: Understanding Your Child's Emotions

Empathy's Role

Empathy, at its core, is about more than merely recognizing the emotions of others—it's about genuinely feeling with them. In the context of parenting a child with ADHD, empathy transforms your approach from one of correction to connection. It allows you to perceive the world as your child does, providing insights into why they may react impulsively or fail to focus. Neuroscientific research shows that empathy strengthens the neural pathways in your child's brain linked to emotional regulation. By consistently responding to your child with compassion, you help them develop the parts of their brain responsible for managing emotions, leading to improved behavior and emotional responses over time.

Seeing the World Through Their Eyes

It's crucial to actively attempt to see situations from your child's perspective to foster empathy effectively. This requires consciously stepping back from your immediate reactions and considering your child's unique challenges. For instance, a simple task like organizing their room can feel overwhelming to a child with ADHD due to difficulties with executive function. Understanding this can help you recognize that their reluctance isn't laziness but a symptom of their condition. Strategies to assist with this include spending a day attending to tasks precisely as your child would, using their organizational systems and schedules. This experiential insight can be eye-opening, providing a clearer understanding of your child's daily hurdles.

Communicating Understanding

Once you've gained a deeper understanding of your child's experiences and emotions, the next step is effectively communicating this understanding back to them. This communication should affirm that their feelings are valid and understood, regardless of how small or irrational they might seem. For example, if your child is frustrated with a seemingly easy homework assignment, acknowledging their feelings by saying, "It sounds like this homework is tough for you right now," can be more validating than simply encouraging them to finish the task. Such validations convey that you are attuned to their feelings and are there to support them, not just to push them to complete tasks.

1. **Active Listening:** You should give your child full attention when speaking. This means maintaining eye contact, nodding, and avoiding interruptions. Demonstrating that you are fully engaged shows you value your child's feelings and thoughts.
2. **Reflective Dialogue:** You should reflect on what you heard your child say. This involves paraphrasing or summarizing your child's words and emotions. For example, "It sounds like you're feeling really upset because your friend didn't invite you to the party."

3. **Validating Emotions:** You should acknowledge and validate your child's feelings without judgment. This means expressing understanding and acceptance of your child's emotions, such as, "It's okay to feel sad and frustrated. Your feelings are important."

4. **Sharing Personal Experiences:** You can share similar experiences and emotions, which helps build a connection and shows everyone experiences identical feelings. For example, "I remember feeling left out when I wasn't invited to a party when I was your age."

5. **Problem-Solving Together:** Encourage a collaborative approach to solving problems. Ask open-ended questions to guide your child in thinking about possible solutions, such as, "What do you think we can do to make you feel better?" or "How can we handle this situation together?"

6. **Modeling Empathy:** You should consistently model empathetic behavior in your interactions with others. Children learn by observing, so when they see you demonstrate empathy, they are more likely to emulate that behavior.

Empathy and Discipline

Integrating empathy into discipline is perhaps one of the most challenging yet rewarding aspects of parenting a child with ADHD. It involves shifting from a punishment mindset to one of teaching and guiding. When a child with ADHD acts out, it's often a response to feeling overwhelmed or misunderstood. Instead of an immediate reprimand, try understanding what emotion drives the behavior. Is it anxiety, frustration, or something else? Once you identify the emotion, you can address it directly, perhaps by discussing what's bothering them or helping them find a solution to their problem. This approach helps resolve the immediate behavior more effectively and teaches your child valuable skills in identifying and managing their emotions. This process is not easy. Children with ADHD are not always sure what their feelings are or why they did something terrible. My son used to cry when being punished, and when asked why he did it, he would say, "I don't know." At the time, that was not good enough for me because I didn't understand emotional dysregulation. I would punish him, and the behavior would constantly repeat itself. We could never understand why he would repeat his behavior. I didn't know he wasn't processing feelings or right from wrong like my other kids. Remember, this strategy takes time to master. Be patient and give yourself grace if you struggle a bit or often. Understanding rather than reprimanding is not something you probably had to do much in your life. This is work for both of you.

Incorporating empathy into your parenting toolkit doesn't just ease the day-to-day challenges—it builds a foundation of trust and understanding that supports your child's emotional and social development. As you continue to apply these empathetic strategies, you create an environment where your child feels safe to express themselves and confident in navigating their emotions.

Encouraging Emotional Expression and Communication

Creating a Safe Space

Creating an environment where your child feels safe to express their emotions openly, without fear of judgment, is like building a foundation of trust and understanding that dramatically benefits their emotional health. This safe space is physical and emotional, where your child knows their feelings are valid and will be heard. You need to encourage your child to express positive and negative emotions freely. For example, you could have a daily "check-in" time where each family member shares their feelings or thoughts. These check-ins should be respected and uninterrupted, showing that everyone's feelings deserve attention.

Introducing expressive activities can also be a highly effective way to help children with ADHD communicate their emotions. For younger children, drawing can be a potent tool; they can draw their feelings or use colors to represent different emotions. Chapter 2 has links for my emotional regulation coloring books on Amazon for kids under 12. It allows children to identify their feelings and gives them time to color that corresponding image, allowing them time to calm down or share more efficiently. Older children might find journaling more helpful, enabling them to explore their feelings more deeply and reflect on why they feel a certain way. Music, whether playing instruments or listening to different types of music, can also help express and manage emotions. These activities provide immediate outlets for emotional expression and build skills that can help children manage their feelings independently in the future.

Normalizing Emotions

It is vital to normalize all emotions. Children with ADHD often experience intense emotions and might feel ashamed or confused about why they feel so strongly. By discussing emotions openly, you validate their feelings and teach them that it's sometimes okay to feel sad, angry, or frustrated. You can use examples from books or shows to illustrate these points, discussing characters' emotional reactions to various situations and asking your child how they might feel in a similar scenario. This helps make the conversation more relatable and enhances your child's understanding of their emotions in a safe and controlled environment.

The Impact of Praise on Self-Esteem and Behavior

Praise vs. Encouragement

In the delicate world of parenting a child with ADHD, understanding the subtle yet profound effects of praise versus encouragement is crucial. While praise often focuses on the outcome of an action, encouragement emphasizes the effort and process regardless of the result. When done effectively, praise can be a powerful tool, enhancing self-esteem and motivating desired behaviors. However, the key lies in how it's delivered and the intent behind it. Specific, descriptive praise goes beyond generic comments like "Good job!" It involves pointing out precisely what your child did well. For example:

- "I noticed you remembered hanging up your coat and putting away your shoes. That really helps keep our home clean."
- "I really liked how you shared your toys with your sister today. That was very kind."
- "You did a great job solving that math problem. I noticed you worked really hard on it!"
- "You worked really hard on your homework tonight, and I can see how much you've improved!"
- "I'm proud of how you kept trying even though that puzzle was tricky."
- "You're getting better at reading every day, and I love hearing you practice!"
- "Seeing you help out without being asked shows how responsible you've become."

This type of praise is more meaningful and helps your child clearly understand what behaviors are appreciated and why. It ties their actions directly to positive outcomes, reinforcing their under-standing of cause and effect, a concept that can sometimes be challenging for children with ADHD.

Guarding Against Over-Praise

However, it's essential to be mindful of over-praise. When praise is given excessively, it can lead children to rely on external validation rather than developing their sense of self-worth and accomplishment. Over-praise can dilute the significance of genuine praise and may lead children to become less self-motivated or to doubt the sincerity of any praise they receive. To avoid these pitfalls, ensure that praise is meaningful and tied to specific actions or behaviors. It should be given when genuinely earned and not used to control behavior or keep a child happy.

Praise For Intrinsic Motivation

Praise should be used strategically to build intrinsic motivation, which is the drive to do something because it is inherently interesting or enjoyable. This involves recognizing and rewarding internal qualities such as persistence, creativity, or kindness rather than just external achievements. For example, praising a child for continuing to work on a challenging task, even if they haven't completed it, helps them value perseverance and self-improvement. This kind of praise encourages children to pursue their interests and challenges for the satisfaction they get from the activity rather than for an external reward.

Chapter 4
Creating a Supportive Home Environment

"When little people are overwhelmed by big emotions, it's our job to share our calm, not join their chaos."

— L.R. Knost

Navigating the daily life of a child with ADHD can feel like trying to solve a puzzle where the pieces keep changing shape. It's a dynamic challenge requiring patience, understanding, and an excellent strategy to bring peace and progress to your child's life and your family dynamics. In this chapter, we focus on a critical part of this strategy: creating a supportive home environment through the power of routine. The goal is not just to manage the symptoms of ADHD but to create an atmosphere where your child can thrive, feeling supported and empowered. By implementing these strategies, you can take control of the situation and feel more confident in helping your child.

Creating a Calming Home Environment: Tips and Tricks

In the busy dance of daily life, a home serves as a sanctuary, a place where each family member can relax and recharge. For a child with ADHD, a calming home environment is essential for their ability to unwind and manage their symptoms effectively. By minimizing sensory overload and creating spaces that encourage concentration and relaxation, you can provide a supportive setting that eases the daily challenges of ADHD. This brings a sense of relief, knowing your home is a safe and calm space for your child.

Reducing Sensory Overload

Imagine a world where every sight, sound, and texture feels amplified. For children with ADHD, particularly those with sensory sensitivities, the typical household environment can quickly become overwhelming, leading to heightened anxiety or behavioral issues. To mitigate this, address the clutter that often dominates our living spaces. A cluttered room not only distracts but also increases stress levels. Implementing a minimalist approach doesn't mean stripping away personality from your home—it's about choosing and arranging elements that serve a purpose or bring joy without overwhelming the senses.

The choice of colors in your home can also play a crucial role in creating a calming environment. Opt for soothing, earthy tones or soft pastels that envelop the room in tranquility rather than vibrant colors that might overstimulate. Similarly, managing noise can help in reducing sensory overload. Consider using white noise machines or soft background music to mask disruptive sounds. When concentration is paramount, such as during homework or relaxation exercises, noise-canceling headphones can be invaluable, allowing your child to retreat into a cocoon of calmness despite the chaos that might reign outside their sanctuary.

Designing ADHD-Friendly Spaces

Each space in your home can be optimized to support the needs of a child with ADHD. Start with the homework area—a space that demands high concentration. This area should be well-lit, preferably with natural light, and equipped with a comfortable, ergonomically designed workspace free from distractions. Simple organizational tools like labeled bins for school supplies and color-coded folders can help maintain order and independence.

It is equally important to create quiet zones in your home where your child can unwind and manage their emotions. These areas should be away from the high-traffic parts of the house and include elements like a cozy bean bag, a shelf with favorite books, or a small tent filled with soft pillows for a sensory break. These dedicated spaces signal to your child that it's okay to take time for themselves to regroup and recharge. Encouraging regular use of this space can teach your child valuable skills in self-regulation—a critical component in managing ADHD symptoms effectively.

Moreover, every item in your home should have a designated place, and this is where specific storage solutions come into play. Use labels on drawers and bins not just to establish where items belong but also to encourage your child to participate in keeping the home organized. This not only aids in reducing visual clutter but also instills a sense of responsibility and accomplishment.

The Power of Routine: Creating Structure and Stability

Establishing a Daily Routine

For children with ADHD, the world can sometimes feel like an overwhelming place, full of distractions and disruptions that can lead to anxiety and a sense of chaos. Consistency and predictability can create a sense of security and control for children with ADHD. Establishing a straightforward routine using visual schedules can help manage expectations and transitions between different activities throughout the day. For example, you could start with a morning routine that includes waking up, getting dressed, having breakfast, and brushing your teeth. These schedules could be as simple as a series of pictures or icons on a whiteboard that outline the day's tasks, from brushing teeth to homework time. They provide a visual reminder that helps keep your child on track without constant verbal prompts.

The benefits of a routine extend beyond just emotional stability. For instance, structured homework time helps your child understand that there is a set time and place for studying, which can improve concentration and decrease procrastination. Similarly, regular meals and bedtimes can help regulate their body clocks, often disrupted in children with ADHD, improving overall health and mood stability. By integrating consistent routines into your child's daily life, you're helping manage their symptoms and teaching them valuable management skills that can benefit them throughout life. Knowing that you successfully implement beneficial strategies for your child can bring a sense of accomplishment.

Flexibility Within Structure

While the importance of a structured routine cannot be overstated, infusing this structure with a degree of flexibility is equally important. Children with ADHD often experience high levels of impulsivity and unpredictability in their behavior, which means that too rigid a routine can become a source of frustration and stress, both for your child and for you. The key is to find a balance that allows for the necessary structure while also accommodating the dynamic needs of a child with ADHD. If your child is resistant to the routine at first, try to involve them in the planning process or offer small rewards for following the schedule. Remember, it's a learning process for both of you, and making adjustments along the way is okay.

This flexibility might mean having a basic framework for the day that includes time blocks for various activities but also allows for choices within those blocks. For example, your child might decide whether they want to do their reading before or after their playtime in the afternoon, giving them a sense of control and ownership over their schedule. This approach helps them learn to manage their time and priorities, crucial skills for children with ADHD, who often struggle with executive function tasks.

Visual Schedules and Timers

Visual aids like schedules and timers can be invaluable in effectively implementing a routine that works for your child. Visual schedules provide a clear and constant reminder of what the day holds, which can help reduce anxiety and resistance to transitions between activities. These can be simple charts with pictures for younger children or more detailed planners for older children, displayed in a common area of the house that your child can easily refer to throughout the day.

Timers are another helpful tool, especially for tasks your child might resist or feel anxious about, such as doing homework or getting ready for bed. Setting a timer for these activities can help your child know exactly how long they'll be expected to focus on a task, making it feel more manageable and less open-ended. This can particularly help with time management, a common challenge for those with ADHD, by visually and audibly signaling the passage of time.

Positive Reinforcement: Encouraging Desired Behaviors

Positive reinforcement is a cornerstone strategy in behavior management, particularly effective in supporting children with ADHD. This approach involves adding a rewarding stimulus following a desired behavior, making the behavior more likely to occur again. For children with ADHD, who may struggle with self-regulation and consistently performing desired behaviors, positive reinforcement can be a powerful tool to highlight successes and encourage their repetition.

Why Positive Reinforcement is Effective

The effectiveness of positive reinforcement in managing ADHD behaviors is well-documented in psychological research. Studies have shown that when children with ADHD receive immediate and consistent feedback for positive behavior, there is a noticeable improvement in their ability to maintain these behaviors. This is particularly significant in educational settings where sustained attention and task completion are often challenging. Rewards do not need to be substantial or material; frequent verbal praise or a small token can be incredibly effective. The key is the positive acknowledgment of the effort and achievement, which fosters a sense of accomplishment and motivation.

Examples of Positive Reinforcements

Examples of effective positive reinforcers vary widely, but they share the common goal of being meaningful to the child. For some, verbal praise is highly effective, while others might respond better to tangible rewards such as stickers, extra playtime, or a small treat. Privileges like choosing a movie on family night or selecting a game for everyone to play can also serve as significant incentives. It's crucial to tailor these rewards to what motivates your child individually. For instance, if a child values social interactions, earning extra time to play with friends can be a powerful motivator. On the other hand, for children who cherish creativity, the opportunity to engage in a preferred creative activity after completing homework can be an excellent reinforcer.

Consistency is Key

Consistency in applying positive reinforcement is crucial for its success. This means that once a reward system is established, it needs to be consistently implemented to reinforce the desired behavior effectively. For instance, if a child earns a sticker for completing homework without reminders, this should be acknowledged every time it occurs to strengthen the behavior. Inconsistency can lead to confusion and diminish the impact of reinforcement, as the child may need to see the link between their behavior and the reward. Maintaining a regular reinforcement schedule helps establish clear expectations and a reliable feedback loop, which is particularly important for children with ADHD who benefit from predictable and structured environments.

Avoiding Overstimulation

However, while implementing positive reinforcement, it's essential to avoid overstimulation. Children with ADHD can become easily overwhelmed if too many rewards are offered or if rewards are too stimulating or distracting. This can decrease the desired behavior, as the child may become more focused on the reward than the behavior itself. To prevent this, choose reinforcers that are exciting enough to motivate but not so engaging that they detract from the primary goals. For instance, if using screen time as a reward, it might be wise to limit it to appropriate times that do not interfere with bedtime or homework. Additionally, the type of reward should be varied occasionally to maintain its effectiveness, as the same reward can lose its appeal over time, reducing its motivational impact.

The strategic use of positive reinforcement helps children with ADHD understand and feel good about their successes. This fosters a positive self-image and a more motivated attitude toward challenging tasks. By thoughtfully applying this approach, you can help your child develop a stronger foundation for self-regulation and positive behavior, essential skills for lifelong success.

Setting Boundaries and Expectations: A Guide for Parents

Understanding the science behind setting clear and consistent boundaries is pivotal in managing children with ADHD. Such boundaries provide a framework of security and predictability, which is instrumental in helping these children navigate their daily lives. Neuroscientific research suggests that children with ADHD often experience difficulties with executive function, which includes challenges in following rules, organizing tasks, and controlling impulses. Clear boundaries help mitigate these issues by establishing set limits and rules that aid in structuring their environment, making it less chaotic and more predictable. This predictability helps in reducing anxiety, which is common in children with ADHD, as they are better able to understand what is expected of them and what they can expect in various situations.

Communicating Clear Expectations

Communicating clear expectations is critical to ensuring that children with ADHD understand the boundaries set and the reasons behind them. This communication should be clear, concise, and consistent, using language that matches the child's level of understanding. Explaining the 'why' behind each rule or expectation is essential, as this helps the child see the purpose behind the boundaries, making them more likely to follow them. For instance, rather than simply stating a rule like "no interrupting when someone is speaking," explain that this helps everyone feel listened to and respected, which is essential for good conversations. Visual aids, such as charts or illustrated lists, can be particularly effective in reinforcing these rules, providing a visual reminder to help children with ADHD remember and adhere to the boundaries.

Appropriate and Predictable Consequences

Moreover, setting consequences for not meeting these expectations is essential to boundary-setting. Consequences should be fair, appropriate, and predictable, designed to teach rather than punish. For example, if a child does not complete their homework, a consequence could be losing some screen time or having extra study time to catch up on what was missed. These consequences should be linked to the specific behavior to help the child understand the direct results of their actions, reinforcing the learning of appropriate behaviors. Importantly, consequences should be consistent; if a rule is broken, you should apply the agreed-upon consequence each time to strengthen the knowledge and establish a reliable structure.

Continuing to Provide Emotional Support

Balancing discipline with emotional support is crucial in fostering a healthy, trusting parent-child relationship. Discipline should be administered to support learning and growth rather than creating fear or resentment. This approach involves showing empathy, understanding, and recognizing that mistakes are part of learning and growth. When a boundary is crossed, take the time to discuss what happened and why it was a problem, and explore together how to handle the situation better in the future. This helps correct the behavior and strengthens the emotional connection between you and your child, as they feel supported and understood rather than judged and punished. It's about guiding rather than dictating, helping your child learn self-regulation and responsibility.

In practice, this balanced approach means being firm but kind, setting clear expectations, and supporting your child as they work to meet them. It involves communication, consistency, and compassion—recognizing that each child is unique and that learning and growth happen at different paces. For children with ADHD, who often face more challenges in navigating social expectations and rules, having the support and understanding of their parents is invaluable. It provides a secure base from which they can explore, learn, and grow, making the boundaries you set together stepping stones to greater confidence and independence.

Fostering Emotional Connections

The emotional connection between you and your child is the bedrock upon which their development rests. Mindfulness strengthens this connection by fostering an environment of open communication and mutual respect. It involves acknowledging and validating your child's feelings, even when they are difficult to understand or manage. This validation helps your child feel safe to express their emotions, knowing they won't be dismissed or judged harshly. An evidence-based approach to mindfulness has shown that such emotional attunement can help improve children's social skills and relationships with peers, which are often areas of difficulty for those with ADHD. This journey towards mindful parenting isn't about perfection; it's about making a conscious effort each day to connect with your child meaningfully. Engaging mindfully enriches your parental experience and profoundly influences your child's emotional and psychological development.

Chapter 5
Creating a Harmonious Home Environment

"It is not what you do for your children, but what you have taught them to do for themselves that will make them successful human beings."

— Ann Landers

Encouraging Independence: Skills for Daily Living

Building Life Skills

Instilling practical life skills such as time management and organization in a child with ADHD transcends daily routines; it lays the groundwork for lifelong self-reliance and success. Children with ADHD often struggle with executive functions, which can make tasks that require planning, organizing, and prioritizing overwhelmingly challenging. Therefore, teaching these skills is not just about improving current behavior but equipping your child with the tools they need to navigate the complexities of life both now and in the future.

These skills are so critical. Effective time management can transform an overwhelming school day into manageable, successful moments. Good organizational skills can turn the chaos of a cluttered study space into a calm, productive learning environment. These competencies are foundational; they help mitigate the daily stresses associated with ADHD by providing a sense of control and predictability. Moreover, they foster self-esteem and competence, which are particularly crucial for children frequently facing academic and social challenges due to their ADHD symptoms.

Step-By-Step Guidance

Offering step-by-step guidance is pivotal in teaching children with ADHD how to approach and manage tasks. Breaking down tasks into smaller, manageable steps can demystify what might initially seem overwhelming and provide a clear path to completion. For instance, if the task is to clean their room, you might break it down into 1) Put all the toys in the toy box. 2) Place books back on the shelf. 3) Put dirty clothes in the laundry basket. Each step is achievable independently, and completing each step provides a sense of accomplishment, encouraging them to tackle the next one. Remember, with ADHD comes processing disorders. This means they may need one step at a time. If you give them three steps, they may not remember steps one and two. Children with ADHD tend to remember the last thing they hear. This may frustrate you, so give them the steps one at a time.

This method can be applied to virtually any task, from homework assignments to getting ready for school in the morning. Visual aids, such as checklists or picture schedules, can enhance this strategy by providing a tangible reminder of what each step entails. These tools guide your child and gradually teach them how to break down tasks independently, fostering independence and building confidence in their abilities to manage their responsibilities.

Celebrating Milestones

Recognizing and celebrating milestones in independence is crucial in reinforcing these new skills and motivating your child to maintain and extend them. Each achievement, no matter how small, is a building block in their journey toward self-reliance. Celebrations can be simple acknowledgments or small rewards that highlight the importance of what they have achieved. For instance, completing a week's worth of homework assignments on time could be marked by a particular family dessert, a movie night, or an extra half-hour of playtime.

These celebrations do more than just reward behavior; they reinforce the child's understanding of the value of their new skills and the positive outcomes they bring. They help build a positive identity as someone capable and reliable, countering any negative perceptions they may have internalized about their abilities due to their ADHD.

Using Technology as an Aid

In today's digital age, technology offers innovative tools that can support children with ADHD in developing independence. Numerous apps and devices are designed to improve organization, time management, and task completion. For example, timer apps can help manage time effectively, providing visual and auditory cues that keep a child on track. Organizational apps can help manage school assignments and deadlines, reducing the chaos that often leads to homework stress.

Moreover, technology can be tailored to fit individual needs, providing customized support that can evolve with your child's growing skills. It's essential, however, to choose and use technology thoughtfully. The goal is to enhance skills, not replace them. Please encourage your child to use technological tools as part of a broader strategy to improve their independence, integrating them with traditional methods like physical checklists and schedules. This integrated approach ensures that your child benefits from the best of both worlds: the conventional skills of organization and the modern efficiencies of technology.

Cultivating a Growth Mindset in Your Child

Fostering a growth mindset is a key part of parenting, especially for children with ADHD. This idea is based on the belief that abilities and intelligence can grow with dedication and hard work. For children with ADHD, this mindset can be very powerful. It changes the focus from seeing skills as fixed and unchangeable to seeing them as things they can develop. Challenges then become opportunities for learning and personal growth.

Stay Positive

The relevance of a growth mindset for children with ADHD cannot be overstated. Often, these children face repeated setbacks in academic and social settings, leading to a fixed mindset—where they might believe that no effort can change their situation. By consciously cultivating a growth mindset, you help your child understand that every effort they make contributes to their development, regardless of the immediate outcome. This understanding can liberate them from the fear of failure, which is often a significant barrier to trying new strategies or persisting through challenges. For instance, when a child who struggles with attention during class lessons is encouraged to see each attempt to focus as a step toward improving their concentration skills, the process becomes a part of their growth rather than a repeated failure.

Encourage Resilience

Encouraging resilience in your child involves more than just urging them to 'keep going' after a setback. It requires a nuanced approach where failures are reframed as essential learning opportunities. This reframing can be achieved through regular discussions about what was learned from each experience and how it can be applied in the future. For example, if a project doesn't go as planned, instead of focusing solely on the outcome, guide your child to reflect on what parts of the project were challenging and why, what strategies they used, and how they might approach it differently next time. This reflective practice builds resilience and enhances problem-solving skills, making your child more adept at navigating future challenges.

Teach Adaptability and Problem-Solving

Moreover, teaching adaptability and problem-solving is crucial. Children with ADHD often encounter situations where their first approach may not work. By teaching them to be adaptable, you prepare them to pivot and try new strategies. Problem-solving sessions can be incorporated into daily routines. These involve discussing potential strategies for homework tasks, planning how to manage transitions between activities, or even strategizing to improve personal relationships. During these discussions, the importance of flexibility and creativity in approach is emphasized, illustrating how each problem presents an opportunity to learn something new about themselves and their environment.

Effort Over Achievement

Lastly, celebrating effort over achievement is critical in reinforcing a growth mindset. This practice helps children understand that value lies in the effort and learning process, not just the end result. It encourages them to engage in tasks focusing on personal development and mastery rather than fear of failure or solely achieving success. When a child, for example, spends considerable effort organizing their room or completing a difficult assignment, recognizing the effort (regardless of how long it took or the imperfections in the outcome) fosters an internal motivation to keep improving. This recognition should be specific and descriptive, highlighting the aspects of their effort that were particularly effective or creative.

Through these practices, cultivating a growth mindset in children with ADHD becomes a transformative tool, turning everyday challenges into growth, learning, and self-discovery opportunities. It prepares them to navigate their current circumstances with more resilience and adaptability. It equips them with skills that will serve them in academic, social, and professional contexts. As you integrate these strategies into your parenting approach, they not only enhance your child's development but also enrich your own experience as you witness every small step of progress they make, knowing it contributes to their more extensive journey of growth.

The Importance of Morning Routines for ADHD

A smooth morning often sets the tone for the day, especially for a child with ADHD, where predictability and structure help mitigate morning chaos. Preparing as much as possible the night before—a strategy often overlooked—can significantly simplify your mornings. This preparation might involve laying out clothes, packing school bags, preparing lunches, and setting out breakfast items. This reduces the number of tasks in the morning and decreases the sensory overload for your child, making the start of the day less stressful and more manageable. Involving your child in this preparation can further enhance their organizational skills and sense of responsibility. For example, asking your child to choose and set out their clothes for the next day can foster independence and decision-making skills while ensuring they feel comfortable and prepared for the day ahead.

A wise person once told me she never spoke angrily or poorly to her child in the morning. She always wanted to contribute to starting the day right for her child because school was stressful enough. Her child said she appreciated that and felt this was the best parenting skill available. Mornings are tough. They become very frustrating, as we all know, but remember that your child will be stressed all day long on school days. Try not to contribute to that stress.

Consistent Routines

A clear and consistent morning routine is crucial for children with ADHD, who often find great comfort and security in knowing what to expect. Establishing a routine and calmly guiding your child through morning activities can help avoid the stress and rush that often lead to meltdowns or forgotten tasks. This routine should include ample time for each activity, from waking up to leaving the house, and be visually displayed in a common home area. Utilizing charts or boards where steps are checked off can provide a visual reminder of the routine, helping your child navigate their morning with greater ease and less reliance on parental prompts. Moreover, these visual cues can help reinforce the sequence of activities, gradually building a habit that can lead to increased independence.

Fostering Empowerment

Empowering your child through choice is another subtle yet powerful strategy that can transform your morning routine. Allowing your child to make simple decisions, such as choosing between two breakfast options or selecting a book to read on the drive to school, can provide them with a sense of control and agency, which is often lacking in the lives of children with ADHD.

This empowerment can lead to increased cooperation and a smoother morning routine flow. It's essential, however, to limit the choices to avoid overwhelming your child. Too many options can lead to decision fatigue, which can be counterproductive and derail the morning routine.

Time Buffers

Another critical aspect to consider is the incorporation of time buffers. Children with ADHD often perceive time differently and may move at a pace that isn't aligned with typical expectations. Building extra time into the morning routine can accommodate this unique pace and reduce the pressure and stress of having to rush. These buffers ensure ample time for your child to complete each task without anxiety, making the morning routine more relaxed and manageable. For instance, if it typically takes your child ten minutes to get dressed, plan for fifteen. This extra time can alleviate the rush and frustration that often accompanies mornings, making the start of the day more pleasant for everyone involved.

Homework Strategies That Work: Reducing Frustration for Both of You

Timing and Structure

Creating a productive and frustration-minimized homework routine for your child with ADHD involves more than just setting aside time for study. It requires a thoughtful approach, where you work together to establish practices that cater to their specific needs and learning styles. This collaboration is essential because children with ADHD often face unique challenges that can make traditional homework routines ineffective. For instance, difficulties with sustained attention and task initiation can turn homework time into a daunting ordeal. To counter this, start by setting a consistent schedule for homework that aligns with the times when your child is most alert and least distracted. This might be right after a light snack and some physical activity in the afternoon, which can help manage energy levels and improve focus.

Once the timing is set, involve your child in creating this routine. This could mean discussing how to break homework into manageable segments or choosing which subject to start with. Engaging them in this planning process makes the routine more tailored to their preferences and enhances their commitment to follow through. Moreover, using tools like planners or homework apps can help your child track assignments and deadlines, fostering a sense of control and responsibility. These tools should be simple and user-friendly, providing enough structure without becoming overwhelming. Some examples are:

myHomework Student Planner:
- Features: Assignment tracking, class schedules, reminders, and calendar integration.
- Platforms: iOS, Android, Windows, Mac, and web.

Todoist:
- Features: Task management, project organization, due dates, reminders, and collaboration tools.
- Platforms: iOS, Android, Windows, Mac, and web.

Study Bunny:
- Features: Timer for study sessions, to-do lists, tracking study progress, and customizable bunny character as a motivational tool.
- Platforms: iOS and Android.

My Study Life:
- Features: Class schedules, assignment tracking, exam reminders, and cloud synchronization.
- Platforms: iOS, Android, Windows, and web.

TickTick:
- Features: Task management, calendar integration, reminders, recurring tasks, and collaboration tools.
- Platforms: iOS, Android, Windows, Mac, and web.

School Assistant:
- Features: Track homework, tests, and schedules, scan documents, see and save Google classroom assignments, and quickly access saved websites.
- Platforms: iOS and Android.

Location, Location, Location

Designating a specific area for homework is another critical strategy. You should tailor this space to your child's sensory preferences, which can significantly impact their ability to focus. For some children, a quiet, minimally decorated space might be necessary to minimize distractions. For others, background music and a more casual seating arrangement might be more conducive to concentration. Your child should consistently use this space for homework to establish a routine, but it should also be flexible enough to change if specific setups are ineffective. It is vital to create an environment that enhances focus and minimizes the sensory overload that can be so disruptive for children with ADHD.

Incorporating Breaks

Breaks are another vital aspect of a successful homework routine. Children with ADHD often benefit from scheduled breaks to help manage their energy and attention spans. These breaks should be planned and structured; for instance, a five-minute break after every 20 minutes of work. During these breaks, encourage activities that allow your child to get up and move around, which can help dissipate restlessness and renew focus. Activities like stretching, jumping jacks, or walking around the house are practical. Keeping these breaks concise and supervised is crucial to ensure your child returns to their homework refreshed and ready to continue.

Collaboration and Communication with Teachers

Collaborating with your child's teachers is also essential to ensure that homework assignments are clear and manageable. Open communication with teachers can help you understand assignment expectations and learning objectives, which you can discuss with your child. If specific assignments consistently cause confusion or frustration, don't hesitate to ask teachers for clarification or modification. This collaboration can lead to adjustments such as reduced homework loads or alternative assignments that align better with your child's learning abilities and reduce stress for both of you. Before my child's official diagnosis, we would spend three hours doing the homework that took other kids 10 minutes. This time was filled with tears from both of us. I was re-teaching every concept to my child, and he still did not understand. It was not until I had a parent-teacher conference, mind you, three months into school, that we discussed this struggle. She suggested spending twenty minutes max on the assignment. If he didn't finish it, then stop. Write a note and put it back in his backpack. We began having a parent folder with a journal where I could explain what happened during homework time. That was a game-changer for me. It made me understand that I did not have to make my son a perfect student in 1st grade. For him, doing two problems was just as hard as others doing ten. He learned through completing those two problems; he would no longer be learning if I made him do the other eight. When the mind is overwhelmed, it is hard to concentrate. Please keep this in mind when pushing your child during homework time.

Implementing these strategies requires patience and flexibility. Each child with ADHD is unique, and what works for one might not work for another. The key is to be observant and responsive—ready to adjust strategies as you learn more about what helps your child succeed. This dynamic approach, combined with consistent support and encouragement, can transform homework from a stressor into a manageable—and even rewarding—part of your child's daily routine. By fostering a structured yet flexible homework environment, you empower your child to overcome challenges and develop the skills they need to succeed academically.

The Art of Time Management for Kids with ADHD

Teaching Time Awareness

For children with ADHD, the concept of time can often feel abstract and elusive. Unlike adults who have developed an internal clock, many children, especially those with ADHD, struggle to grasp how long tasks take, leading to frustration and time mismanagement. To aid your child in becoming more time-aware, start by tangibly discussing the concept of time. Use situations they are familiar with, such as the length of a favorite TV show or the time it takes to eat a meal, to begin understanding different time intervals.

A practical method to teach time management is through role-playing various scenarios. For instance, you could set up a game where your child needs to complete a simple task, like building a block tower, within a set time limit. Use a timer to make this exercise more concrete, and discuss with them afterward how long they felt the task took versus the actual time. This type of exercise makes them more aware of passing time and engages them in understanding time estimation in a fun and interactive way.

Visual Timers and Clocks

Visual timers and clocks are invaluable tools for helping children with ADHD comprehend and manage their time effectively. These tools provide a visual representation of time, which is often more understandable for children than numbers on a clock. Visual timers that show the passing of time with a red disc or a digital countdown can help children see how much time they have left to complete an activity, which can be a powerful motivator and an anxiety reducer.

Incorporate these timers during homework sessions, playtime, or while preparing to leave the house. For example, setting a timer for 20 minutes during homework can visually cue your child on how much time they have to focus before taking a break. This keeps them informed and provides a structured framework to manage their activities.

Clocks with features that teach time concepts, like color-coded hours, minutes, and seconds, can also be placed in your child's bedroom or study area. These are tools for telling time and educational aids that reinforce daily time-telling lessons, making time management a consistent part of their environment. Something to keep in mind is that some children with ADHD get anxious with time. If this is the case for your child, visual timers may not be appropriate.

Prioritizing Tasks

Learning to prioritize tasks is a critical skill for children with ADHD, who often feel overwhelmed by multiple responsibilities. Teach your child to distinguish between urgent tasks and those that are important but not immediately necessary. This can be done by creating a 'priority list' together, where tasks are categorized into 'must do,' 'should do,' and 'nice to do.'

For practical application, use visual aids like a color-coded chart or sticky notes on a board where tasks can be moved from one category to another, providing a clear visual of priorities. This method helps in organization and makes abstract concepts of priority more concrete and manageable.

During this exercise, engage your child in thinking about the consequences of not completing tasks in each category. For example, not doing homework (a 'must do') might mean they are unprepared for school the next day and may result in not going out for recess, or if older, resulting in a Saturday detention, whereas not playing a video game (a 'nice to do') might mean slightly disappointing. Through these discussions, your child develops critical thinking about the importance of tasks, which is fundamental in mastering prioritization. The Eisenhower Decision Matrix is a helpful tool for deciding what is important and what is not important at the time.

Eisenhower Decision Matrix

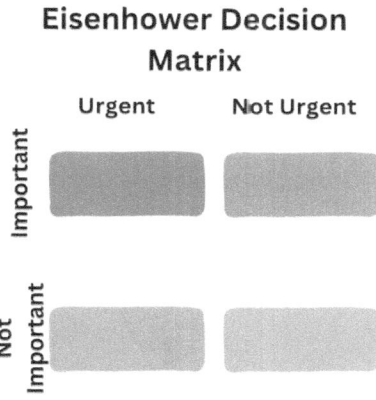

Rewarding Punctuality and Task Completion

Reinforcing positive time management behaviors through rewards can be a strong motivator for children with ADHD. Establish a system where punctuality and timely task completion are consistently recognized and rewarded. This could be as simple as praise after your child gets ready for school on time or a small reward like extra reading time before bed if they finish their homework by the set time.

Additionally, consider creating a 'time management chart' where your child can earn stickers or tokens for successful time management. At the end of the week, these tokens can be exchanged for a larger reward. This system provides immediate motivation and feedback and helps build long-term habits by linking consistent effort with positive outcomes.

By integrating these strategies into your daily routine, you are helping your child become more proficient in managing their time and instilling skills that will serve them well throughout their academic and personal life. Time management for children with ADHD isn't just about getting to places on time or finishing tasks; it's about building a framework within which they can feel more in control, less stressed, and ultimately more confident in managing the complexities of daily life.

Managing Screen Time: Balancing Technology and Activity

In today's digital age, screen time is an inevitable part of children's lives, especially for those with ADHD, who may find the fast-paced feedback of digital media particularly engaging. However, managing screen time is crucial, as excessive use can exacerbate ADHD symptoms such as inattention and impulsivity. Striking a balance requires setting realistic and enforceable limits that respect your child's needs and technology's benefits.

Setting Limits

Setting adequate screen time limits involves understanding the unique needs of your child. Children with ADHD often experience time differently; what feels like a few minutes can turn out to be an hour. Therefore, clear, consistent guidelines about when and how long they can use screens are crucial. Using evidence-based guidelines from pediatric health sources can provide a framework, but it's important to tailor these recommendations to your child's circumstances. For instance, while the general recommendation might limit screen time to one or two hours per day for children, you might find that your child functions best with a bit more or less, depending on their daily activities and managing their ADHD symptoms. For my son, video games exacerbated his anger and frustration. I found a phonics game that included putting out fires in a building, as you answered the question correctly. My son loved fire trucks and would spend his screen time on this "video game," which no longer caused that frustration. It was a fun game that helped him with his reading—another game-changer. Be creative.

It's also beneficial to involve your child in setting these limits. This could mean discussing together what reasonable screen time looks like and having them help set up a schedule that includes time for homework, physical activity, and relaxation. This involvement makes the limits feel more self-directed, fostering a greater sense of responsibility and adherence and teaches them essential planning and negotiation skills.

Rewards or Consequences?

Using screen time as a reward is a common strategy, but it has pros and cons that need careful consideration. On the positive side, screen time can be a powerful motivator for children with ADHD. For example, earning screen time to complete homework or chores can reinforce positive behaviors and provide a clear incentive. However, the downside is that this can make screen time the most coveted activity, overshadowing other valuable pursuits like reading or playing outside. It can also lead to bargaining behavior or meltdowns when access to screen time is denied or limited based on behavior. Therefore, if you choose to use screen time as a reward, it is crucial to set clear, consistent rules about how much screen time can be earned and ensure that it is part of a balanced array of rewards that includes non-screen activities.

Incorporating Active Play

Encouraging active play is essential, particularly for children with ADHD. These children often need to burn off excess energy and can benefit from physical activity's focusing effects. Balancing screen time with active play can help mitigate some of the hyper-activity and impulsivity associated with ADHD. Activities for active play include a quick game of tag, a family bike ride, or a sit-up challenge with family members in the living room. These activities provide necessary physical exercise, strengthen family bonds, and create joyful shared experiences.

Alternating Educational Technology

Lastly, the educational use of technology should be considered. Many apps and programs are specifically designed to aid learning and development. For children with ADHD, these tools can offer engaging ways to practice academic skills or learn new information. For instance, educational apps that gamify math or reading skills can engage your child and make learning feel more like play. Choosing well-designed apps with evidence supporting their educational value is essential, ensuring that screen time is fun and enriching. Keeping up-to-date with the latest reviews and recommendations for educational technology can help you make informed choices that enhance your child's learning experiences. Chapter 10, *"Technology in Education: Tools for Success,"* mentions suggestions for highly-rated apps.

Incorporating these strategies into your screen time management creates a balanced digital diet that respects your child's attraction to screens while prioritizing their overall development and well-being. By setting clear limits, using screen time judiciously as a reward, encouraging physical activity, and selecting educational content thoughtfully, you can ensure that screen time is a positive addition to your child's daily routine. This balanced approach not only helps manage the potential negative impacts of screen time on ADHD symptoms but also leverages technology for engagement and learning, reflecting the complexities and opportunities of raising children in the digital age.

The Importance of Sleep: Strategies for Better Nights

Sleep Challenges in ADHD

Understanding why sleep poses such a challenge for children with ADHD is critical because it lays the foundation for why we need tailored strategies to manage it. Research indicates that children with ADHD often have difficulties with the internalization of circadian rhythms—the internal clocks that dictate our sleep-wake cycles. This disruption manifests as problems in falling asleep, staying asleep, and sometimes waking up too early or at irregular intervals. Neurological studies suggest that this may be due to irregular secretion of melatonin, the hormone that regulates sleep, and an overactive central nervous system that struggles to calm down. The result is a child who feels physically tired but whose brain cannot settle into the quiet state necessary for deep sleep. This lack of restorative sleep can exacerbate common ADHD symptoms such as inattention, impulsivity, and emotional volatility, setting a challenging cycle into motion where sleeplessness feeds into daytime behaviors, which, in turn, disrupt sleep further.

Establishing a Bedtime Routine

Creating a calming bedtime routine is like preparing the ground for planting—it's about making the right conditions for growth, or in this case, restful sleep. Start by setting a consistent bedtime based on your child's natural sleepiness cues. This consistency helps reinforce the body's sleep-wake cycle, making it easier for your child to wind down over time. The routine leading up to this set bedtime is just as crucial. Activities such as a warm bath, reading a favorite book together, or doing gentle stretches should be soothing and predictable. These activities signal your child's brain that it's time to slow down. Keeping the hour before bed low stimulation—avoiding vigorous play and electronic screens, which can emit blue light that interferes with melatonin production—is essential. Instead, focus on quiet, comforting interactions that foster a sense of safety and relaxation.

Impact of Poor Sleep

The repercussions of inadequate sleep extend beyond groggy mornings. Studies have shown that poor sleep can significantly worsen the symptomatology of ADHD, impairing cognitive functions such as attention, memory, and problem-solving. It also affects emotional regulation, making it harder for your child to manage frustration and control impulses, leading to more conflicts and stress within the family. Moreover, chronic sleep deprivation can impact physical health, including immune function and metabolism, affecting overall well-being and growth. This cascade of effects shows why addressing sleep issues is not just about improving sleep itself but about enhancing the overall quality of life for your child and your family.

Sleep Hygiene Practices

Optimal sleep hygiene involves creating practices that promote regular, restful sleep patterns. For children with ADHD, this includes rigorous adherence to routines and creating a sleep-conducive environment. Ensure that the bedroom is used only for sleep and relaxing activities so it becomes a strong cue for sleep. The room should be cool, quiet, and dark—blackout curtains and white noise machines can be helpful tools. Also, consider the impact of diet on sleep—limiting caffeine and sugar intake throughout the day and ensuring a balanced evening meal can prevent dietary impacts on sleep quality. Regular physical activity during the day can also promote better sleep, but stimulating activities should be avoided close to bedtime.

The Sleep Environment

Creating an optimal sleep environment is central to improving sleep for a child with ADHD. This involves more than just a comfortable bed. The entire atmosphere of the bedroom should encourage relaxation. Wall colors should be soft and muted, bedding should be relaxed and breathable, and clutter should be minimized to reduce overstimulation. Each child might have specific needs; some might need a weighted blanket for added security, while others might prefer multiple soft pillows. Personalize the space to suit your child's preferences, involving them in the choices to give them a sense of control and comfort with their sleep space.

Addressing Sleep Disorders

If you've optimized bedtime routines and sleep environment and your child still struggles with sleep, it might be time to consider that a sleep disorder could be at play. Conditions like sleep apnea, restless legs syndrome, or insomnia are more prevalent in children with ADHD. For example, sleep apnea can cause significant sleep disruption and daytime fatigue. At the same time, restless legs syndrome can make it difficult for your child to fall asleep due to uncomfortable sensations in their legs. Consult with a pediatrician or a sleep specialist if you suspect such issues. These professionals can conduct appropriate assessments, such as sleep studies, to diagnose and treat underlying conditions. This is crucial because addressing these can sometimes lead to significant improvements in both sleep and ADHD symptoms.

Limiting Stimulants

Finally, managing the intake of stimulants is crucial in the hours leading up to bedtime. This includes apparent stimulants like caffeine and less obvious ones like certain foods and activities that can energize the brain. High-sugar snacks, stimulating TV shows, or exciting video games close to bedtime can all make it harder for your child's brain to wind down. Replace these with calming snacks like a glass of warm milk or light reading, and encourage quiet activities like puzzles or drawing to help ease the transition into sleep.

Fostering Independence Through Routine

Independence is not just about doing things independently; it's about owning the process and feeling capable. For children with ADHD, building independence through daily routines offers a structured way to enhance their self-efficacy and self-reliance. The key here is gradual progression—allowing your child to take on more responsibility at a pace that acknowledges their unique challenges yet pushes towards growth. This step-by-step guidance on fostering independence supports their developmental needs and empowers them to manage their ADHD more confidently.

Delegating Tasks

Start with identifying areas of your child's daily routine that offer opportunities for taking on more responsibility. This could be anything from organizing their school bag to managing their laundry. Begin by breaking down these tasks into smaller steps and clearly outlining what success looks like for each step. For instance, if the task is to organize their school bag, the steps might be: 1) Empty the bag completely. 2) Sort the contents into 'keep' and 'discard.' 3) Organize the 'keep' items back into the bag, with each item in its designated spot. Walk through these steps with your child initially, guiding them as they learn to manage each part. As they become more comfortable and competent, gradually reduce your involvement, allowing them more autonomy to complete the task independently.

Acknowledging Success

Celebrating each milestone of independence is crucial. It reinforces the value of your child's efforts and bolsters their motivation to tackle more complex tasks. Acknowledgment can be as simple as verbal praise, a high five for younger children, or something more formal, like a chart where they earn stickers for each task they manage independently. These celebrations act as powerful affirmations of their capabilities, counteracting any frustrations or self-doubt they might encounter due to their ADHD symptoms. It's about creating a positive feedback loop where success breeds more success, which is especially important for children who might often encounter negative feedback in other areas of their lives.

Incorporating Problem-Solving

Problem-solving skills are essential for independence, especially for children with ADHD, who may frequently encounter situations where routines are disrupted. Teaching them to identify problems, think through possible solutions, and decide on the best course of action is a critical life skill. Start by modeling this process yourself. For example, verbalize your thought process if you're running late in the morning: "We're running late because we couldn't find your shoes. Next time, we could lay out your shoes the night before. What do you think?" This shows them how to approach problems and involves them in the solution, making the learning process interactive and practical. Gradually, encourage them to develop solutions independently, guiding them with questions rather than providing answers.

Tools for Independence

Introducing tools for independence can also play a transformative role. Checklists are a simple yet effective tool that can help manage daily tasks. These can be visual checklists with pictures for non-readers or written lists for older children. Place these checklists in strategic locations, like on the refrigerator door or next to their bedroom light switch, as reminders of what needs to be done. Alarms can also be helpful, especially for time-sensitive tasks. Teach your child to set alarms on a clock or a smartphone, which can be an independent reminder for starting or stopping activities, such as homework or screen time. These tools aid in task management and building a routine that doesn't rely heavily on parental prompts, fostering a sense of independence and self-regulation.

Celebrating Successes: Recognizing Small Wins

Acknowledging every small achievement in your child's life is critical in shaping their self-esteem and motivation, especially for a child with ADHD. These children often face frequent challenges and setbacks, making it imperative for you as a parent to spotlight every victory, no matter its size. Recognizing these wins reinforces their efforts and instills a sense of accomplishment, significantly boosting their willingness to tackle new challenges. This positive reinforcement is vital, as it shifts focus from what they struggle with to what they excel in, fostering a healthier self-image and a more optimistic outlook toward life's hurdles.

Creating a Family Culture of Celebration

Creating a culture of celebration within the family unit sets a powerful precedent. It teaches all members to recognize and value success in themselves and others, fostering an environment of support and appreciation. This culture goes beyond acknowledging achievements related to significant milestones like grades or sports victories. It includes everyday successes, such as managing emotions well during a stressful situation or completing chores without reminders. To cultivate this culture, make it a habit to share successes at the dinner table, allowing each family member to highlight something positive from their day. These sharing moments strengthen the family bond and reinforce a collective identity rooted in mutual support and recognition.

Personalized Reward Systems

Personalized reward systems are an effective strategy to make success tangible, especially for children with ADHD, who may need external cues to help them connect actions with outcomes. These systems should consider what motivates your child and align rewards with their interests and achievements. For instance, if your child excels in a task they usually find challenging, like organizing their room, a related reward could be going out for ice cream after dinner. Alternatively, if they have been working on managing interruptions, a reward might be choosing what the family has for dinner that night. The key is to ensure these rewards feel meaningful to the child and directly correlate to their efforts and accomplishments.

Chapter 6
The Impact of ADHD on Sibling Relationships

"Fairness is not giving everyone the same thing. Fairness is giving each person what they need to succeed."

— Rick Riordan

Understanding Sibling Dynamics

The presence of ADHD within a family can uniquely stress sibling dynamics. Siblings of a child with ADHD might experience a range of emotions, from jealousy due to the perceived extra attention the child with ADHD receives to neglect, as parents often have to devote significant time and energy to managing ADHD-related challenges. These feelings, if not addressed, can lead to frustration and conflict. However, understanding these dynamics is the first step toward fostering a supportive family environment.

Recognizing the Feelings of All Family Members

It is crucial to recognize each child's feelings and give them the attention and support they need. This can be achieved through consistent communication, ensuring all children have space to share their thoughts and feelings. Listening actively to their concerns can help mitigate feelings of neglect or jealousy and promote equality and understanding within the family. Educating siblings about ADHD is fundamental. It helps demystify the behaviors associated with ADHD, such as impulsivity or difficulty following tasks, which siblings might otherwise perceive as intentional or irritating. By explaining that these behaviors are symptoms of ADHD and not deliberate choices, siblings can better understand the challenges their brother or sister faces.

Fairness and Attention: Balancing Family Dynamics

In a home where ADHD plays a significant role, the challenge of distributing attention equitably among siblings can often seem daunting. Each child, with unique needs and personalities, requires time and energy, which can fluctuate daily depending on numerous factors. This dynamic can inadvertently lead to feelings of unfairness or neglect among siblings. It's crucial to employ strategies that ensure each child feels valued individually and appreciates their role within the family unit.

Balancing Attention

Balancing attention among siblings starts with a conscious effort to spend quality one-on-one time with each child. This might mean scheduling specific dates with each child, where the activities align with their interests. For example, if one child enjoys art, planning an afternoon of painting or visiting a local gallery can make them feel special and appreciated for their unique preferences. Similarly, if another child is sports-oriented, attending their games or having a catch in the park can be significant. These moments are opportunities to connect on a deeper level, allowing each child to feel seen and heard without the shadow of ADHD defining the interaction. It's about making each child feel important in their own right, which can significantly reduce any resentment stemming from the divided attention that is sometimes necessary when managing ADHD.

Expectations for All

Managing expectations across the board is another pivotal element. Children with and without ADHD come with different sets of capabilities and challenges, and it's essential to set realistic expectations for each child's behavior and contributions. This might involve recognizing that a child with ADHD might need more reminders to complete chores or homework, whereas a sibling might be more self-directed. Communicate these expectations clearly and adjust them as your children grow and their capabilities change. This approach helps minimize frustrations and misunderstandings, fostering an environment where children feel they are treated fairly according to their abilities and not unequally.

Be Fair

Creating clear family rules and routines that accommodate the needs of all members is crucial in promoting a sense of fairness and cooperation. This could involve establishing routines that incorporate the strengths and interests of each child, allowing them to contribute in ways that make them feel competent and valued. For instance, a child who enjoys cooking might be responsible for helping with meal preparation once a week. In contrast, a child who excels in organization might assist in planning family outings or gatherings. Such roles encourage responsibility and highlight each child's contributions to family life, reinforcing their importance to the family's overall dynamics. For me, we began snowmobiling as a family. My son with ADHD is mechanically inclined and good at operating large vehicles/trailers. When we planned a trip and my one son was in sports and unavailable to help prepare, we would have my son with ADHD help prepare the snowmobiles, park the snowmobiles in the trailer, hook up the trailer to the truck, etc. This sense of accomplishment made him feel good about his contributions to the family trip and provided him with solid skills for jobs he held in the future.

Everyone Deserves Recognition

Celebrating individual and collective family accomplishments fosters unity and mutual support. This practice can be as simple as acknowledging personal milestones like a good grade or a new skill learned and celebrating achievements involving the whole family, such as completing a group project or enjoying a successful family outing. These celebrations can be marked during family meetings or meals, ensuring everyone's contributions are recognized. Highlighting these successes reinforces that while each person may shine independently, the family's greatest successes come from working and supporting each other, fostering a strong sense of team spirit and collective price.

Incorporating these strategies into daily family life ensures that each child feels valued for who they are, understands their unique contributions to the family, and recognizes the importance of supporting each other. This balanced approach not only addresses the individual needs of children with and without ADHD but also strengthens the family unit, making each member feel integral to the family's success and harmony.

Creating Inclusive Family Activities

Family activities are the bedrock upon which memories are built, and bonds are strengthened. For families juggling the dynamics associated with ADHD, creating inclusive activities that cater to both the child with ADHD and their siblings is not just beneficial —it's essential. In fostering teamwork and collaboration, consider activities that inherently require working together towards a common goal. Building a model rocket, planning a family garden, or even cooking a meal together are activities that not only necessitate cooperation but also teach valuable social skills such as shar-ing, turn-taking, and collective problem-solving. These activities encourage siblings to see each other as teammates rather than competitors. For a child with ADHD, working in a team can be particularly instructive; it teaches them about structure and social cues within a safe and supportive environment. Moreover, it provides a shared sense of accomplishment once the task is completed, which can be incredibly affirming.

Adapting Activity for Inclusion

Adapting activities to ensure inclusivity is another crucial consid-eration. This might involve modifying the rules of games to accommodate shorter attention spans or incorporating more breaks during family outings. If you plan a movie night, for exam-ple, choose engaging but not over-stimulating films, keeping in mind the sensory sensitivities that can accompany ADHD. Similarly, when planning a day out, consider locations that are not overly crowded or noisy, which can be overwhelming for a child with ADHD, and ensure there are quiet spaces to retreat to if needed.

Chapter 7
Enhancing Social Skills

"In teaching children how to interact with others, we are teaching them how to navigate the world."

— *Unknown*

Navigating the playground, understanding unspoken cues in the classroom, or simply sharing a toy can be very hard for a child with ADHD. ADHD often involves impulsiveness, difficulty paying attention, and trouble reading social cues, which can make social interactions challenging. What seems easy for other kids can feel like a complicated puzzle for children with ADHD. As a parent, it can be heartbreaking to see your child struggle with these social challenges. However, with the right strategies and understanding, you can turn these challenges into chances for growth and connection.

Social Skills Training: Making Friends and Fitting In

For children with ADHD, social interactions aren't just challenging; they're crucial battlegrounds for personal development. These children often face hurdles in reading facial expressions or body language, making it challenging to grasp social nuances. Their impulsivity may lead to interrupting conversations or reacting without thought, behaviors that can confuse or push away potential friends. Understanding these challenges is the first step in helping your child navigate the complex world of social interactions. By recognizing that these difficulties are part of the condition, not a reflection of their desire to connect or make friends, you can approach their social skills training with empathy and precision.

Communication Challenges

Children with ADHD often struggle with fundamental aspects of communication, such as maintaining a topic of conversation or interpreting the tone of voice, which are critical in everyday interactions. These challenges can lead to misunderstandings and frustrations on both sides of a conversation. However, by explicitly teaching and practicing communication skills in controlled environments, you can help your child become more proficient and confident in their ability to communicate. For example, role-playing various social scenarios at home can provide your child with a safe space to practice turn-taking, staying on topic, and interpreting non-verbal cues.

Structured Social Skills Programs

Structured social skills training programs can be beneficial for children with ADHD. These programs teach and reinforce necessary social skills systematically, often through group sessions where children practice with each other under the guidance of a trained professional. The benefits go beyond just learning skills; children also develop more empathy as they learn to understand and consider others' feelings and improve their conflict resolution skills. These programs often use fun methods like storytelling, games, and role-playing to keep children interested and enthusiastic. Here are some resources to connect with social skills programs that are highly recommended. These resources are to spark your mind with programs out there that you may have to look for in your area. Remember, Chapter 1 lists national organizations that can direct you to a local chapter of these organizations.

1. **Second Step Programs:** This platform offers a range of social-emotional learning programs for children from pre-K through high school. These programs focus on nurturing positive relationships, managing emotions, and achieving goals, thus helping children thrive in school and life settings (Second Step).
2. **PEERS® by UCLA's Semel Institute:** This evidence-based social skills program is designed for preschoolers, adolescents, and young adults and specific contexts like

dating and career skills. PEERS is renowned for helping individuals improve their social communication skills, including making and keeping friends, understanding social cues, and managing social interactions (Semel UCLA) (Patient Care at NYU Langone Health).

3. **TeachTown Social Skills:** This program offers an interactive curriculum for younger children, particularly those with special needs. It focuses on teaching appropriate social behaviors through videos, social skills worksheets, and lesson plans that cover various behavioral domains such as communication, coping, and friendship (PositivePsychology.com).

4. **Child Mind Institute's PEERS® Program for Young Adults:** This 14-week intervention is designed to help motivated young adults develop better social skills to make and maintain friendships. It involves group therapy sessions where participants learn various social skills, including engaging in conversations, managing social interactions, and developing long-lasting friendships (Child Mind Institute).

Practical Social Skills Activities

You can engage in numerous activities at home to bolster your child's social skills. Simple games that require turn-taking can teach patience and fairness, while activities that involve following complex instructions can improve listening skills. Empathy-building exercises can enhance your child's ability to empathize with others. Consider discussing the emotions of characters in a book or movie. Use apps designed to improve social skills, such as "Social Adventures" or "The Social Express," which provide interactive scenarios and feedback. Write different emotions on cards and have children act them out without using words. Other participants guess the emotion, which helps children learn to recognize and interpret feelings. Create scenarios where children practice introducing themselves, starting conversations, and making friends. Be cautious of only giving your child one suggested statement about introducing themselves or starting conversations. I was at a family reunion once, and one child said the same statement to everyone he met, drawing attention to his neurodiversity. Give many different options and work on who your child should say which statement to. Act out situations where children need to resolve conflicts or disagreements positively. Role-play everyday social situations, like saying "please" and "thank you" or asking for help politely. Any of these activities bolster social skills, which are important for future growth.

Building Communication Skills

Effective communication is foundational to successful social interactions. Encouraging your child to express their thoughts and feelings clearly and listening to them attentively when they do models the kind of communication you hope to see from them. Additionally, you can help your child develop conversation skills by guiding them on how to start a conversation, ask open-ended questions, and stay engaged by showing interest in what others say. Encouraging reading and storytelling can expand your child's language skills and give them the tools to express themselves more effectively. Discussing stories and asking questions about motives and feelings can further enhance their language proficiency and ability to navigate social situations. These skills, practiced regularly at home, can significantly improve your child's ability to interact positively with peers.

Encouraging Positive Peer Interactions

Creating opportunities for your child to interact with peers in a structured, supervised setting can foster positive social experiences. Organizing playdates, encouraging participation in group activities, or enrolling your child in clubs that align with their interests can provide them with the safe social settings they need to practice their skills. These interactions can be pivotal in helping your child make friends and fit in, significantly boosting their confidence and social competence. One thing I learned, however, was it was best to do activities that were planned as play dates. For instance, my son was interested in playing with matchbox cars, whereas his friends were interested in sports. Activities such as bowling, hiking, or going to a park allowed him to develop social skills without having my son's interests conflict with his friends' interests.

In helping your child develop social skills, remember that each small step forward is a giant leap in their ability to connect with others. Your child can handle social interactions more smoothly and confidently with your support, understanding, and active involvement. As you use these strategies, you'll likely see an improvement in your child's social skills, self-esteem, and overall happiness.

Dealing with Bullying: Strategies for Parents and Children

Bullying is an issue that no child should have to endure, yet it remains a harsh reality for many, particularly those who might appear different, such as children with ADHD. Due to their unique behavioral traits, such as impulsivity and the potential for social awkwardness, children with ADHD may unfortunately find themselves more frequently targeted by bullies. Recognizing the signs of bullying can often be challenging. They don't always manifest through visible scars; they can also appear as changes in behavior, sudden drops in academic performance, or unexplained withdrawals from social interactions. Staying attuned to subtle shifts in a child's demeanor or routine can be crucial as a parent. For instance, an eagerness to avoid school or a particular setting where they previously displayed comfort can be a potential indicator. Furthermore, listen actively to the child's casual conversations; mentions of being picked on or teased, even in passing, should prompt further gentle inquiry.

Teach Anti-Bullying Skills

Empowering your child to deal with bullying effectively is critical. This involves fostering a sense of self-assurance and teaching them strategies to stand up for themselves. Role-playing can be helpful here; it allows your child to practice responding to negative interactions in a safe environment. Teach them firm, straightforward ways to assert themselves verbally, such as saying "stop" clearly and confidently or "Don't. I don't like what you are saying." It's also important to stress the value of seeking help when the situation escalates beyond their control. Ensuring they understand there is no shame in reporting bullying to an adult is essential for their safety and well-being.

Communicate with School Staff

Communication with schools plays a pivotal role in combating bullying. A partnership with a child's educational institution is essential to fostering a safe learning environment. Start by familiarizing yourself with the school's anti-bullying policies and the procedures for reporting incidents. Schedule meetings with teachers, counselors, and administrators to discuss your concerns and establish clear lines of communication. During these discussions, advocate for specific actions that can be taken to protect your child, such as increased supervision during recess, lunchtime, or any other times they are more vulnerable. Additionally, inquire about school programs that educate students about bullying and promote inclusiveness. Being proactive and involved with the school empowers you to act swiftly should incidents occur and helps ensure that the school is a supportive partner in addressing and resolving these issues.

Building Resilience

Building resilience against bullying is one of the most empowering tools you can equip your child. This involves nurturing their self-esteem so that they are less likely to be affected by others' negative words or actions. Celebrate their strengths and accomplishments regularly, and provide them opportunities to succeed and feel competent, whether in academics, hobbies, or social scenarios. Encourage them to foster friendships with supportive peers, as these relationships can provide emotional support and bolster their confidence. Additionally, consider engaging your child in activities promoting resilience, such as martial arts, which can improve physical and psychological strength.

As we wrap up this discussion on managing the challenges of bullying, it's clear that a proactive, informed approach is essential for safeguarding your child's well-being. Recognizing the signs, empowering your child, effectively communicating with schools, and building resilience are all strategies that contribute to a supportive environment where your child can thrive despite the challenges posed by bullying.

Extracurricular Activities: Finding the Right Fit

Extracurricular activities offer experiences that can significantly enrich your child's life, especially for those with ADHD. The benefits are multifaceted: from boosting self-esteem as they master a new skill to finding joy and passion in activities that resonate with their interests. These activities also serve as crucial outlets for their boundless energy. They provide structured opportunities to practice social interactions in a more relaxed setting than school offers.

Matching Interests with the Activity

When considering extracurricular activities for your child, the key is to find the right fit—a task that involves more than just matching activities to their interests. It requires a thoughtful assessment of how the structure and pace of the activity align with your child's unique needs. For instance, a child who thrives in fast-paced environments might excel in sports like soccer or basketball, where quick decisions and movements are integral to the game. On the other hand, a child who does better in less chaotic, more predictable environments might find joy and success in martial arts or swimming, where routines are consistent, and the focus is often on individual performance rather than team dynamics. Do not choose the activity based on what you want for your child. I made that mistake many times. My older son played football, basketball, and baseball. I put my son with ADHD in football, and he was only able to understand the special teams plays. I put him in basketball, and he could only understand how to play defense. Offensive plays were tough for him. Baseball was okay because, in baseball, he only needed to understand one to two things at a time. As I look back on the videos of him playing football and basketball, I feel very guilty for putting him in activities that meant a lot to my husband and me. Don't get me wrong, he thoroughly enjoyed being a part of a championship team, and it taught him other essential skills, but I do not believe that sport was his choice. Eventually, he asked to learn to play the guitar and thrived. It is imperative to consider their type of ADHD and what their interests are.

Consider the Social Environment

The social environment of the activity is equally critical. Consider whether the activity fosters a supportive, inclusive atmosphere. It's beneficial to choose programs where instructors are knowledgeable about ADHD and are committed to fostering an environment where all children, regardless of their challenges, are encouraged and valued. This support is crucial in helping your child feel secure and accepted, which are key factors influencing their enjoyment and continued participation in the activity. Again, my son was playing football, practicing six days a week as a five-year-old, and only getting into the game for the kickoff. He had to stand there for the rest of the game. It was heartbreaking. The coaches were very competitive and did not understand his inability to catch onto plays. Instead of working with him, he was dismissed.

Communicate with Activity Leaders

Working with activity leaders is vital to ensure that your child's experience in extracurricular activities is positive and enriching. Communication with coaches, instructors, and other leaders can make a significant difference. Discuss your child's strengths and challenges openly, providing insights into what strategies work best for keeping them engaged and focused. I was confused at that time about my son's ability, and I never advocated. Advocating is very important. For instance, if your child benefits from visual cues, a coach can be encouraged to use visual aids when explaining new concepts or strategies. Similarly, if transitions are challenging, activity leaders can be asked to provide clear warnings when one activity ends and another begins.

I was a coach for 28 years. I had many children with learning disabilities and diagnoses. Parents needed to communicate with me about their child's needs and how they learned. Once I had that information, I was more patient with them and taught them how they could understand. Do not be afraid to advocate. It provides less stress on your child and their activity leader.

Make Sure the Activity is Not Too Much

Balancing these activities with academic responsibilities is crucial to keeping your child calm. It involves practical time management and setting realistic expectations about what is manageable. Start with one activity to gauge how much additional structure your child can comfortably integrate into their routine without impacting their school responsibilities or family time. Monitor their stress levels and enjoyment, and be ready to make adjustments. This balance is not static; it requires flexibility and ongoing dialogue with your child to find the right mix of activities that provides enrichment without exhaustion.

By thoughtfully choosing and managing extracurricular activities, you create opportunities for your child to discover new passions, develop essential skills, and build confidence in social settings. These experiences are invaluable, providing your child with a sense of accomplishment and belonging that fuels their growth and happiness.

Chapter 8
Ensuring Your Child Thrives in Educational Settings

"Never underestimate the power of a parent's voice. Your advocacy can change the course of your child's life"

— Unknown

N avigating the educational rights and accommodations for a child with special needs can feel daunting, but understanding these pathways is crucial to ensuring your child succeeds and thrives in their academic environment. This chapter is dedicated to demystifying the structures in place—particularly Individualized Education Plans (IEPs) and 504 Plans—and guiding you through securing the support your child deserves.

Understanding Educational Rights: IEPs and 504 Plans

Clarifying the Differences

The landscape of educational support is populated with various forms of assistance, but two primary vehicles provide access to tailored education strategies: the Individualized Education Plan (IEP) and the 504 Plan. Both plans are designed to assist students with disabilities, yet they cater to different needs and are governed by different laws. An IEP, established under the *Individuals with Disabilities Education Act (IDEA)*, provides specialized educational services to children who meet specific criteria for one of 13 categories of qualifying disabilities, which include ADHD under certain conditions. It's a legally binding document that outlines specific educational goals, the services the child will receive, and how progress will be measured. Conversely, a 504 Plan, which falls under the *Rehabilitation Act of 1973*, is less about specialized education and more about ensuring that a student with a disability has equal access to an education. This plan modifies the learning environment and teaching strategies so students can learn alongside their peers, not necessarily through additional educational services but through accommodations like extended time on tests or seating near the teacher. In my career, I have also found 504 plans to include being able to remove themselves from the classroom if they become too stressed or even not attend school on a day when anxiety is at its high. These missed days are excused. There have been issues, however, where children take advantage of this accommodation, so you have to do due diligence as a parent to ensure it's not abused.

Eligibility and Evaluation Process

Determining eligibility for an IEP or a 504 Plan begins with a comprehensive evaluation process that assesses your child's unique needs. For an IEP, this process typically starts with a referral—either by you or a teacher—who notices that the child might not be making adequate progress in the general education setting. Following the referral, the school evaluates to determine if your child has one of the specific disabilities listed under IDEA and needs specialized education. For a 504 Plan, the evaluation looks at whether your child's disability substantially limits one or more major life activities, including learning. This evaluation can include a variety of data sources, including psychological tests, grades, and teacher observations. Your pediatrician may also be able to make a referral to the school for accommodations.

Process of Obtaining Services

Once eligibility is established, the following steps differ slightly between the two plans. For an IEP, if your child is found eligible, you will work with a team of school professionals to develop the plan. This team typically includes teachers, school psychologists, other specialists, and, importantly, your child and you as the parent. The plan outlines specific educational goals tailored to your child's needs and specifies the services required to achieve these goals, such as resource room time or occupational therapy. For a 504 Plan, the process is less formal. Still, it involves a similar team to help determine the necessary accommodations to ensure your child can access the general education curriculum. In both cases, your active participation as a parent is crucial. You know your child best; your insights can help shape a plan that fits their needs.

Creating an Effective Plan

Creating an effective IEP or 504 Plan is a collaborative effort that requires clear communication and thoughtful consideration of the child's strengths and challenges. The key here is specificity and measurability. For an IEP, this means setting clear, achievable goals tailored to your child's unique educational needs, and for a 504, specifying the accommodations that will best support your child's learning. Regular meetings are part of this process, providing opportunities to review progress and make adjustments as necessary. Ensuring that your child is involved in this process, where appropriate, can empower them and help them understand their learning process, which is invaluable as they grow and learn to advocate for themselves.

Accommodations Available for Children with ADHD

The range of accommodations for children with ADHD can be vast, but they should always be tailored to your child's specific challenges and strengths. These might include preferential seating, extended time on tests, reduced homework or classwork, verbal testing, breaks during class, or technology aids. Knowing what accommodations are available and how they can support your child's learning will allow you to advocate effectively for their inclusion in the IEP or 504 Plan.

Your Rights as a Parent

As a parent, you have specific rights throughout the evaluation and planning process. These include the right to request an evaluation, to be part of the team that decides on eligibility and plans, to be informed of your child's progress, and to dispute decisions about your child's education through processes like mediation or a due process hearing. Although the IDEA law does not mandate schools to provide educational advocates, you have the right as a parent or caretaker to have an advocate present if you want to dispute a current plan or follow through with a plan. Parents often seek advocates when they need additional support to navigate the special education system or when disputes arise with the school about their child's education plan. Advocates can be professionals with expertise in education law or volunteers from various advocacy organizations. Parents may need to hire private advocates or seek help from nonprofit organizations that offer advocacy services. For more detailed information and assistance, you can contact local or state advocacy groups, parent training and information centers, or consult an attorney specializing in education law. Awareness of these rights can empower you to be an effective advocate for your child, ensuring their educational environment is one in which they can truly thrive.

Navigating your child's educational rights and accommodations might seem overwhelming, but with the proper knowledge and strategies, you can ensure they get the support they need. This understanding sets the stage for academic success and builds advocacy skills to help you and your child throughout their educational journey. As you move forward, remember that each step you take is a step toward creating an educational experience that honors and supports your child's unique way of interacting with the world.

Advocating for a child with issues with an Individualized Education Program (IEP) or a 504 Plan involves several steps. Here's a guide to help parents navigate this process:

Understand Your Child's Rights:
• Familiarize yourself with the Individuals with Disabilities Education Act (IDEA) and Section 504 of the Rehabilitation Act. These laws ensure that children with disabilities receive appropriate education and services.

Know the Details of the IEP/504 Plan:
• Thoroughly review your child's current IEP or 504 Plan. Understand the specific goals, accommodations, modifications, and services that have been outlined.

Document Everything:
• Keep detailed records of all communications with school staff, including emails, phone calls, and meetings. Maintain copies of all reports, assessments, and correspondence related to your child's education.

Communicate Regularly:
• Maintain open lines of communication with your child's teachers, special education staff, and school administrators. Regular updates and check-ins can help identify issues early on.

Request a Meeting:
• If you notice issues with implementing the IEP or 504 Plan, request a meeting with the IEP team or 504 coordinator to discuss your concerns. Be specific about what's not working and provide examples.

Prepare for Meetings:
- Before any meeting, prepare by listing your concerns, questions, and possible solutions. Bring any relevant documentation and be ready to discuss your child's progress and any obstacles they face.

Be Collaborative but Assertive:
- Approach meetings with a collaborative mindset, aiming to work with the school to find solutions. However, don't hesitate to assert your child's rights and advocate strongly for their needs.

Seek Independent Evaluations:
- If you believe the school's assessments are not comprehensive or accurate, consider seeking independent evaluations from qualified professionals. These can provide additional insights and support your advocacy efforts.

Know When to Seek External Help:
- If you're not progressing, consider seeking assistance from special education advocates, attorneys, or organizations specializing in educational rights. They can provide guidance and support in navigating the system.

Utilize Dispute Resolution Options:
- If disagreements persist, you may need to explore formal dispute resolution options such as mediation, due process hearings, or filing a complaint with the state education agency.

Stay Informed and Educated:
- Continuously educate yourself about special education laws, your child's rights, and best practices in advocacy. Attend workshops, webinars, and support groups to stay informed and connected with other parents.

By taking these steps, you can effectively advocate for your child and ensure they receive the appropriate education and services they are entitled to. The following section will explain in greater detail why using proper communication skills is the most effective way to advocate. Emotions run high when you are worried about your child. Stay calm, be educated, and be prepared before approaching meetings.

Communicating Effectively with Teachers and School Staff

Building Relationships

Building positive, collaborative relationships with your child's teachers and school staff is important for creating a learning environment where your child can thrive, especially if they need special accommodations due to ADHD. Establishing a good relationship based on respect and shared goals helps ensure effective communication and teamwork, essential when adjustments or interventions are needed to support your child's learning and development.

One effective strategy to build a strong relationship with your child's teachers and staff is initiating communication early in the school year. Rather than waiting for the first parent-teacher conference, consider setting up an introductory meeting or sending a brief email outlining your desire to work closely with them. In this communication, express your appreciation for their efforts and share a little about your child's strengths, challenges, and interests. This gives teachers valuable insights into how they might best support your child and positions you as a cooperative and engaged parent. Regular follow-ups, perhaps after each grading period or after significant school events, can help maintain this relationship, ensuring ongoing dialogue and mutual understanding.

How Best to Advocate

When preparing for meetings with teachers or school staff, especially those where you need to discuss concerns or negotiate accommodations, it's crucial to approach the conversation with a clear and constructive mindset. Start by outlining the main points you wish to discuss and consider what outcomes you hope to achieve. Stay focused during the meeting, and use specific examples to illustrate your concerns. For instance, if your child struggles with staying focused during long assignments, describe specific incidents demonstrating these challenges and discuss possible strategies to help manage them. It's also beneficial to ask open-ended questions that encourage discussion rather than simple yes or no answers. Questions like "What strategies do you think could support my child better in class?" or "How can we make homework more manageable for them?" can lead to more productive and creative solutions. Advocacy requires clarity, persistence, and, importantly, a non-confrontational approach. When advocating for specific interventions or accommodations, clearly explain why these measures are necessary for your child's success and back up your requests with observations or, if applicable, recommendations from health care providers or educational psychologists. Sharing strategies that have been effective at home or in previous classroom settings can provide teachers with valuable insights and tools. Regular check-ins can help adjust strategy and ensure accommodations effectively support your child's learning. Always aim for dialogue rather than demand; frame your requests as seeking the best possible outcome for your child, which also benefits the school by enhancing your child's ability to engage and learn. Remember, the goal is to partner with the school staff, so maintaining a respectful and cooperative tone even when negotiations get challenging is critical.

Staying informed and involved in your child's education is more than attending scheduled meetings; it requires active engagement with your child's academic life. This could mean regularly checking in with your child about their day, reviewing homework assignments together, or using school-provided platforms to keep track of educational progress and upcoming events. Many schools now use digital tools like parent portals and mobile apps that provide real-time updates on grades, attendance, and teacher notes. Familiarize yourself with these tools and make them a part of your routine. This keeps you informed and shows your child that you value their education and support their efforts, which can be incredibly motivating for them.

Chapter 9
Preparing for School Transitions

"Change is not something to fear, but something to embrace. Teach your child how new schools bring new friends and new experiences."

— Unknown

I magine standing at the doorway of a new world with your child, filled with colorful crayons, tall storybooks, and the excitement of making new friends. Starting elementary school is a significant milestone in your child's educational journey, full of opportunities and adjustments. For a child with ADHD, this transition isn't just about new backpacks and classroom rules; it's about getting used to a new environment that can be very different from home or daycare. This chapter is dedicated to smoothing this transition, ensuring that you and your child step into elementary, middle, and high school with confidence and a clear plan for success.

Transitioning to Elementary School

Preparing Your Child Emotionally

Preparing your child emotionally for the transition to elementary school involves more than just talking about what school will be like—it's about nurturing resilience and excitement for this new adventure. Begin these conversations months in advance, focusing on the positive aspects of school—such as making new friends or learning exciting things. Use story books or children's shows about school to help paint a vivid picture and relate their upcoming experiences to those of beloved characters. It's also important to validate any fears or anxieties they express, reassuring them that feeling nervous about new experiences is expected. You can role-play different school scenarios, like saying goodbye at the school gate or asking the teacher for help, to build their confidence and equip them with strategies to handle these situations. These role-playing sessions prepare them for what's to come, strengthen their bond, and provide insights into their worries or questions about school.

Visiting the New School

Visiting the new school with your child can ease their anxiety about this significant change. Arrange for a school tour, ideally during a quieter time when the halls aren't bustling with activity, allowing your child to explore their new environment at their own pace. Walk them through the key areas they will use daily, like their classroom, the playground, and the cafeteria. Familiarity breeds comfort; the more they can visualize and physically acquaint themselves with the space, the less intimidating it will feel. Meet their future teacher during the visit to establish a friendly, recognizable face. These visits can transform the unknown into the familiar, making the first day of school much less daunting.

Establishing Routines Early

Routines are particularly crucial for children with ADHD, providing a predictable structure that reduces anxiety and improves focus. Start establishing school-like routines several weeks before school begins. Gradually adjust their daily schedule to mirror the school day, including earlier bedtimes and wake-up times. Introduce visual schedules that outline the daily routine, including morning preparations, travel to school, and after-school activities. These visual cues help reinforce the new schedule and make abstract concepts concrete. Practice these routines consistently to ensure your child feels secure and knows what to expect daily. Familiarizing with the daily flow can make the transition smoother and help them feel more in control.

Collaborating with New Teachers

Building a proactive and transparent relationship with your child's new teacher is vital. Before the school year starts, arrange a meeting to discuss your child's strengths, challenges, and effective strategies that you've observed at home or in previous educational settings. Share insights into what motivates your child, sensory issues, or specific rewards and consequences that resonate with them. This partnership with the teacher ensures they know your child's needs and are prepared to support them effectively from the first day. Regular communication with the teacher will help you monitor your child's adjustment and progress, making addressing potential issues easier.

The Move to Middle School: What to Expect

As your child approaches the transition to middle school, the landscape of their educational environment undergoes a significant shift. This new chapter introduces a more complex structure where they will navigate multiple teachers and classrooms for the first time. The simplicity of having one or two primary teachers who understand their quirks and needs gives way to many educators, each with their own expectations and teaching styles. This can be particularly challenging for a child with ADHD, who may require more time to adjust to changes and learn new routines.

Processing the Expectations

Developing strategies to help your child move between classes and adapt to various teaching methods is crucial to facilitate this shift. Start by fostering a dialogue with your child about what to expect in middle school—highlighting that they will have the opportunity to explore different subjects taught by various teachers can be exciting yet daunting. To smooth this transition, consider creating a 'middle school simulation' experience at home. You can set up different 'stations' around the house, each dedicated to a different subject or activity. Spend short periods at each station, mimicking the movement between classes. This makes switching rooms for different subjects less intimidating and helps your child practice managing their belongings and materials as they move from one activity to another. Most schools arrange for the kids to move up to the next school to do a school visit. This may be enough for children without ADHD, but for a child with ADHD, this is not enough. Reach out to the principal and ask for permission to do a walk-through with your child a few times once their schedule is created. Do it several days, each time having them try to find things themselves. Lockers are daunting. Practice how to get into a locker and how to organize it. Locker organizers can be set up during these visits.

Organization

Organizational skills become even more crucial as your child faces the increased workload and responsibilities of middle school. Teaching your child how to use an organizer or digital planning tools can be a game-changer. Spend time together setting up a system that works for them, be it a traditional binder with different sections for each subject or a digital app that allows them to track assignments and deadlines. The key is consistency and regular check-ins to ensure they use the tools effectively. Another important strategy is to find out which kids of parents you know are in each class so you have someone to call or text to make sure your child understands the assignments. Remember, it takes a village. Finally, encourage them to end each day by reviewing what was accomplished and planning for the next day, boosting their organizational skills and enhancing their sense of control and preparedness.

Social Anxiety

The middle school also brings a new set of social dynamics. The relatively sheltered environment of elementary school expands into a broader social arena with new peers from diverse backgrounds. For a child with ADHD, who may already face challenges in social interactions and maintaining friendships, this can be a daunting prospect. Encourage participation in structured extracurricular activities that provide a safe socialization environment where shared interests pave the way for building new friendships.

How to Teach Self-Advocacy

Lastly, teaching self-advocacy skills becomes essential as your child enters an environment demanding more independence. Middle school is ideal for them to learn how to articulate their needs and seek help when necessary. This skill is particularly critical for children with ADHD, who may need specific accommodations to succeed academically and socially. Start by ensuring your child understands their ADHD, not as a barrier but as a condition that they might learn differently. Help them craft a simple, straightforward way to explain this to their teachers and peers. Practice scenarios where they might need to advocate for themselves, such as asking for extra time on a test or needing a quiet space to complete assignments. My son struggled to know the homework daily because teachers began giving homework assignments verbally instead of writing them on the board. Once my son expressed this issue to the teachers, they began accommodating him by writing it down on the board. Had he not asked for this, this would not have happened, and he would have missed assignments constantly. Empowering your child with the confidence to speak up about their needs is not just about navigating middle school—it's a life skill supporting their self-reliance and success far beyond the school years.

High School and Beyond Preparing for Independence

High school is an important time in your child's life. Schoolwork gets more complicated, and they start to become more independent. High school offers many opportunities and challenges that can shape their future. For a child with ADHD, it's important to prepare carefully, not just for schoolwork but also for learning life skills that will help them as they grow into adulthood.

Difficult Expectations

The academic demands of high school are notably more rigorous than in earlier years. Subjects deepen in complexity, and the volume of assignments can be overwhelming. It's crucial to prepare your child for these challenges by building on organizational and study skills introduced in middle school. Advanced planning becomes essential. Teach your child to use a detailed planner for tracking assignments and deadlines, encouraging them to break larger projects into manageable tasks. Time management strategies are equally important. Introduce techniques such as the **Pomodoro Technique**, where work is broken into intervals with short breaks, which can help maintain focus, reduce feeling overwhelmed, and avoid burnout. This is an excellent technique for studying for tests. Studies show that spreading out study sessions over time and revisiting the material regularly helps improve long-term retention.

- **Choose a Task**: Pick a task you want to work on.
- **Set a Timer**: Set a timer for 25 minutes. This period is called a "Pomodoro," named after the tomato-shaped kitchen timer Cirillo used.
- **Work on the Task:** Work on the task without interruptions until the timer goes off.
- **Take a Short Break:** Take a 5-minute break. Use this time to relax and clear your mind.
- **Repeat:** After four Pomodoros, take a more extended break, usually 15-30 minutes.

Additionally, emphasize the importance of a designated study area free from distractions, where your child can study effectively. If your child cannot pass tests, have your child advocate for study guides, which high school doesn't usually do. My son had to do this, showing his desire to do well. He had a Biology class that was very difficult for him, and he had a rigorous teacher. She did not agree to do study guides, but he advocated for how he wanted to do well, which was the only way he could do it now. She reluctantly created them, and he started to do so much better. He didn't use it as a crutch; he used it as an opportunity to understand the concepts. By the second semester the teacher nominated him for the "Most Improved Student" award. Self-advocating is so important. Regularly revisiting and adjusting these strategies will help your child cope with the increased workload and develop a routine that facilitates academic success.

Getting Involved in Activities

Extracurricular activities play a significant role in high school, offering relief from academic pressures and a chance to explore personal interests and talents. Encourage your child to engage in activities that align with their passions, whether sports, music, theater, or volunteer work. These activities provide a platform for social interaction and skill development. They also offer valuable time management, teamwork, and leadership lessons—skills crucial for personal and professional success. For a child with ADHD, who may sometimes struggle with low self-esteem or social anxiety, succeeding in an extracurricular activity can boost confidence and foster a sense of belonging.

Fostering Independence

Fostering independence in your child is the most crucial aspect of their high school experience. This involves more than just academic preparation; it requires teaching them essential life skills. Focus on decision-making processes by allowing them to make choices about their courses and extracurricular activities. Encourage problem-solving by discussing potential challenges they might face, such as balancing schoolwork and extracurricular commitments, and brainstorming solutions. Self-care is another critical area—teaching them the importance of maintaining their health through proper nutrition, exercise, and sleep, often neglected during this busy phase of their lives. Promoting these skills prepares them for the immediate challenges of high school and lays the groundwork for successful, independent adult life.

Planning for the Future

Discussing post-high school options early in the high school years is vital. Whether your child is interested in college, vocational training, or entering the workforce, understanding the paths available helps them make informed decisions about their future. Discuss the different requirements for each path, such as the need for college preparatory courses or technical skills, and how they align with your child's strengths and interests. Begin exploring potential colleges or training programs and discussing what environments might best support their learning needs. Help your child understand the value of internships or part-time jobs, which can provide practical experience and further clarify their career interests.

Once that decision is made, go full force. If your child wishes to go to college, don't let the stereotype that college is not for kids with ADHD stop you. My son made the decision he wanted to go to college when he was in 8th grade. When we went into his IEP meeting, we realized he was not enrolled in any College Prep courses in high school. The school counselors would not entertain his possibility of succeeding in college. In fact, we had to fight with the Head of Special Education and ultimately sign off on special education to have him "allowed" to enroll in College Prep courses. I am not going to lie; 9th grade was tough. I am sharing this for many reasons, such as because I feel it is important. The first difficulty was that from 2nd-8th grade, most of his day was spent in reading support, math support, and being pulled out of classes for testing. Those accommodations were reasonable, but I never considered the consequences, and I trusted the professionals had his best interest at stake. With those accommodations comes a lack of a need to study as much, so studying skills were not developed. Note-taking wasn't needed because he was always given study guides. Reading a novel wasn't expected of him because he had reduced multiple choice options and many reading prompts. Most detrimental was his close-knit friends stayed in the lower-level classes. As we all know, most of your friend groups are solidified by high school, so when he went into College Prep classes with social skills limited by his ADHD, it was challenging for him to figure out where he belonged. As you will read later in the medication part of the book, his health suffered. But that is neither here nor there. The important thing for you to know is that by 10th grade, things clicked. By 11th grade, he enrolled in dual enrollment at the local community college. By 12th grade, he could also take online classes through high school, and it was as though he was a college student already. He graduated with an Associate Degree, making the Dean's List every semester, and it gave him the confidence to succeed and begin at a non-entry level position in his career. I am unsure where he would be without our dedication to helping him achieve his goals. This may not be the path your child chooses, but whatever that may be, do not be complacent. Stay in tune with your child's goals along the way so they can achieve them!

Chapter 10
Addressing Learning Challenges

"When we equip students with the tools they need, we empower them to unlock their full potential."

— *Unknown*

Enhancing Reading and Writing Skills in ADHD

Reading and writing can be tricky for children with ADHD, with many challenges that might make it hard to enjoy these skills. However, with the proper techniques and tools, you can make the path clearer and more exciting, turning frustrations into chances for growth and discovery. The way to help children improve their reading and writing is by using methods that fit their unique learning styles and build on their strengths.

Reading Comprehension

Improving reading comprehension is crucial because it lays the foundation for academic success across all subjects. Children with ADHD often struggle with attention and may find it challenging to follow narratives or retain information, which can hinder their understanding and enjoyment of reading. To address this comprehension issue, break reading sessions into manageable segments. This method reduces the cognitive load and allows for frequent breaks, which can help maintain focus and engagement. During these reading sessions, encourage active reading by asking questions about the content, prompting your child to make predictions about the story or to summarize what they've read. This interaction keeps them engaged and enhances their understanding and retention of the material. Audiobooks and printed texts can also appeal to different learning senses, aiding comprehension and retention. Listening to the text while following along can help maintain focus, improve language skills, and enhance the reading experience. Most schools have access to these audio programs that allow your child to have the technology post-graduation.

Writing Aids

When it comes to writing, children with ADHD often face challenges such as organizing their thoughts, staying on topic, and following the writing process from brainstorming to final edits. Introducing specialized tools and techniques can make a significant difference. For instance, speech-to-text software can assist those who may have difficulties with handwriting or typing. This technology allows children to express their thoughts fluidly without being hindered by motor skills and can help capture their ideas more effectively. Another powerful tool is graphic organizers, which are visual diagrams that help structure thoughts and ideas. These organizers can take various forms, such as Venn diagrams, story maps, or flowcharts, and serve as a visual framework to guide children through the writing process. By visually breaking down tasks into smaller, more manageable components, graphic organizers can help children with ADHD see the larger picture and connect their thoughts coherently.

Incorporating reading and writing into daily routines is another strategy that can reinforce these skills in a natural, stress-free environment. This practice can be as simple as reading a menu aloud while dining out, writing grocery lists together, or sending thank-you notes to friends and family. These everyday activities offer practical and relatable opportunities for children to practice their skills, making reading and writing part of their daily lives rather than tasks limited to the classroom. Furthermore, this approach helps in demystifying these skills, showing children that they are not just academic exercises but are also functional and integral to everyday communication.

Using these strategies improves your child's reading and writing skills and boosts their confidence and enjoyment of learning. These tools support your child's learning journey, helping them manage ADHD and discover the joy of communicating through words. Each child learns differently, so being flexible and attentive to their needs will give the best results.

Technology in Education: Tools for Success

Technology has become very important in education, offering new ways to help children learn, especially those with ADHD. Assistive technologies, from simple apps to advanced devices, can make learning more accessible for your child by addressing their specific needs. For example, there are apps designed to improve focus and organizational skills, which are often challenging for children with ADHD. Time management apps can help your child see their schedule in a fun and interactive way, making it easier to keep track of assignments and deadlines. Some apps also provide reminders and alarms to help students manage their time better, which is especially helpful for those who struggle with this.

Integrating these technologies into your child's learning plan should be thoughtful and deliberate, ensuring that each tool or app directly contributes to their educational goals. At home, you might start by incorporating educational apps that reinforce core skills, such as math or reading, through interactive and engaging activities that keep your child interested and focused. Many of these apps use gamification to make learning more engaging, providing immediate feedback to help your child understand concepts more quickly and retain information more effectively. Some highly recognized math learning apps for math are Khan Academy, Prodigy Game, Photomath, CK-12, Brightly, and Rocket Math. Some highly recognized reading apps are Epic! Books for Kids, Homer, Starfall Learn to Read, Reading Eggs, Hooked on Phonics, and FarFaria.

Technology can be integrated into the classroom through tablets or computers, allowing customized learning experiences. For example, teachers can use software that adapts to their child's learning pace, offering more practice and review for concepts they find challenging and advancing when they are ready. Sometimes, teachers can substitute written homework assignments assigned to other children with teaching software practice for your child. Do not be afraid to ask.

Digital Organization Tools

Digital organization tools are another aspect of educational technology that can be particularly beneficial for students with ADHD. These tools are convenient and life-changing, helping students keep track of their academic tasks and materials in one accessible and easy-to-manage place. Features like digital calendars, note-taking apps, and cloud-based storage can significantly improve the academic performance of students who struggle with disorganization and forgetfulness. MyHomework Student Planner, Todoist, Study Bunny, My Study Life, TickTick, and School Assistant are highly recommended apps. Chapter 5, *"Homework Strategies That Work: Reducing Frustration for Both of You,"* explains these apps in more detail.

Finding Resources Easily

Staying up-to-date with the latest educational technology is crucial for maximizing its benefits for your child. With AI at your fingertips, you can research any topic you wish, and it will research millions of online information to give you suggestions. ChatGPT is an excellent AI resource for this, and you can use the free version, which will provide you with all you need. Additionally, keep abreast of new tools and apps and continuously assess the effectiveness of current technologies. Regularly check in with your child about which tools they find helpful and which they don't, and be prepared to make adjustments as needed. Additionally, subscribing to newsletters, joining online forums focused on educational technology, or attending workshops can provide insights and updates on emerging technologies and how they are being used effectively in academic settings.

Collaborating with Educators

Collaborating with educators is essential to ensure that technology use is well-aligned with your child's educational goals and any existing plans, such as IEPs or 504 plans. This collaboration can involve regular meetings with teachers to discuss technology integration in the classroom and how it can support your child's specific needs. It's also essential to ensure that any technology used at home complements what is being used in school, providing a consistent and seamless learning experience for your child. This might mean using the same or similar software and apps or coordinating strategies to maximize the use of technology for learning and development.

Incorporating technology into your child's education enhances learning and promotes independence. You can create a supportive and effective learning environment by choosing the right assistive technologies, using these tools at home and school, and keeping in touch with teachers. This approach uses modern technology to meet the unique needs of your child with ADHD.

The Role of School Counselors in Supporting ADHD Students

School counselors are a crucial link between students, parents, and teachers. They are trained to provide counseling that supports students' emotional well-being, which is particularly important for children with ADHD who may experience higher levels of social and emotional difficulties. These difficulties could range from struggles with self-esteem to challenges in forming and maintaining friendships. Counselors can offer one-on-one support or group sessions where children can learn coping strategies, social skills, and more effective ways to interact with their peers. Additionally, counselors often lead or facilitate programs that promote a positive school climate, helping to create an inclusive and supportive environment for all students, including those with ADHD.

Building Relationships

Working effectively with school counselors involves open communication and partnership. Initiate this relationship by scheduling a meeting with the counselor to discuss your child's needs and strengths. During this meeting, share insights about how ADHD affects your child, including any specific triggers or successful strategies used at home. This information can be invaluable as counselors often help develop or modify Individualized Education Plans (IEP) or 504 Plans, ensuring these documents accurately reflect your child's needs and provide appropriate accommodations.

Accessing Resources

Accessing resources is another critical area where counselors can provide significant assistance. They often have detailed knowledge of school-based resources and community services, such as tutoring, social skills groups, or mental health services. For instance, if your child needs help with organizational skills, a counselor can recommend or help facilitate access to school-based tutoring or study skills groups. If emotional challenges are a concern, they may refer your child to a school psychologist or connect your family with external mental health professionals. By fostering a strong relationship with the school counselor, you ensure your child can access various resources designed to support their academic and personal development.

Advocacy and Collaboration

Advocacy and collaboration form the cornerstone of adequate support for students with ADHD. As a parent, your advocacy role involves standing up for your child's rights and working collaboratively with school staff, including counselors, ensuring your child receives the support they need. This collaboration might involve regular check-ins with the counselor and other school staff, participating in meetings, and sharing updates about your child's progress or any concerns. A collaborative approach ensures everyone is aligned on the goals and strategies to support your child. It also fosters a team environment where your child's success is a shared goal, reinforcing the support network surrounding your child.

School counselors can be very helpful in creating a supportive and effective educational environment for your child with ADHD. By understanding their role, working closely with them, using the resources they recommend, and staying collaborative and proactive, you can help your child not only manage their ADHD but also thrive in school.

Parent-Teacher Conferences

Preparation

As you approach a parent-teacher conference, consider it a routine meeting and a pivotal opportunity to engage in your child's academic life actively. These conferences allow you to gain insights into your child's progress, highlight areas where they excel, and discuss strategies for their challenges, particularly those associated with ADHD. To ensure a productive dialogue during the conference, coming prepared is vital. A robust checklist for the meeting should include any relevant reports from outside professionals that provide insights into your child's learning or behavioral needs. These can help the teacher understand the context and expert recommendations surrounding your child's ADHD. Include examples of your child's homework that might highlight specific academic challenges or achievements. These samples can serve as concrete examples to discuss ways to support your child's learning process. Also, prepare a list of questions or observations from home that can shed light on how your child feels about school, which subjects they enjoy most, or any social challenges they are experiencing. This preparation ensures that the meeting covers academic and emotional aspects of your child's school life, providing a holistic view of their well-being.

Communication Skills for Advocating

Effective communication during the conference is vital. Approach the conversation with a mindset that seeks to understand and collaborate. Active listening is essential; pay attention to the teacher's assessments and be open to their observations about your child. This can give you a broader perspective on your child's school experience. When advocating for your child's needs, do so respectfully, framing your requests as a quest for solutions that best support your child's unique learning requirements. For instance, if discussing additional accommodations under a 504 Plan or IEP, explain how specific adjustments could help manage your child's ADHD symptoms more effectively, enhancing their learning potential.

Following up after the conference is just as important as the meeting itself. Outline the steps you will take to implement any agreed-upon strategies or to monitor the progress of new interventions. Setting up a follow-up meeting or agreeing on a communication plan with the teacher can help keep both parties accountable and ensure that the strategies discussed are effectively employed. Keeping detailed notes during the conference and sending a thank-you email summarizing the key points and next steps can reinforce the collaborative relationship and show appreciation for the teacher's efforts.

In wrapping up this chapter, it's clear that active participation in your child's education through strategies like effective advocacy at parent-teacher conferences, understanding and utilizing educational technology, and enhancing reading and writing skills are critical in navigating their learning challenges with ADHD. Each strategy discussed supports your child academically and empowers them with the confidence and skills needed for long-term success.

Chapter 11
The Role of Lifestyle in Managing ADHD

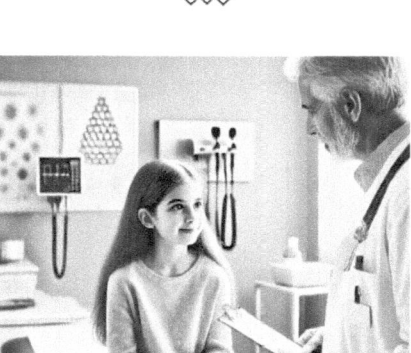

"Wellness is the key to a bright future. Prioritize your child's health to unlock their full potential."

— *Unknown*

I n this chapter, we explore the role of diet in managing ADHD, exploring how certain foods can either exacerbate or alleviate symptoms. This isn't just about avoiding sugar-laden treats or artificial additives; it's about crafting a balanced diet that supports brain health and stabilizes energy levels, creating a nutritional environment that helps your child thrive at home and in school.

ADHD-Friendly Diet: Foods to Embrace and Avoid

Understanding Nutritional Impact

The connection between the gut and the brain is profound, and recent science has shed light on how intertwined they are. The gut-brain is crucial in mood, behavior, and cognitive functions. Certain foods can cause inflammation or imbalances in the gut, which may exacerbate ADHD symptoms. Conversely, a diet rich in certain nutrients can enhance brain function, reduce symptoms, and support overall mental health. Finding the right foods for children is difficult, especially if you are trying to ensure they do not include ingredients that are not good for them, so some ideas below will help.

Foods to Embrace

Focusing on a diet rich in whole foods can be transformative for children with ADHD. Incorporate a variety of fruits and vegetables, as they are high in antioxidants and fibers that aid digestion and brain health. Berries, dark leafy greens, beets, and artichokes are high in antioxidants. Apples, carrots, bananas, and broccoli are high in fiber. Whole grains like oats, brown rice, and quinoa provide complex carbohydrates to fuel an active child's body and mind. Lean proteins such as chicken, turkey, and legumes support muscle growth, brain development, and neurotransmitter functions. Encourage the intake of healthy fats, especially those rich in omega-3 fatty acids, which are crucial for neurological development and can be found in flaxseeds, walnuts, and avocados.

Foods to Avoid

It's equally important to understand which foods might hinder your child's ability to manage their ADHD symptoms. High-sugar foods and simple carbohydrates can cause spikes in blood sugar, leading to hyperactivity followed by a crash in energy and mood. High-sugar foods are sugary drinks, candy and sweets, baked goods, ice cream and frozen drinks, and some processed snacks like packages of granola. Simple carbohydrates are white bread, white rice, pasta, crackers, chips, and cereals with added sugar. You may have heard that artificial colors such as Yellow No. 5, Yellow No. 6, Red No. 40, and Red No. 3, and certain preservatives, such as Sodium Benzoate, in many processed foods have been linked to increased hyperactivity. However, the FDA, after a review in 2011 and reevaluation in 2019, concluded that there is insufficient evidence to claim a definitive relationship between food color additives and increased hyperactivity or ADHD in children. For parents and caregivers concerned about the effects of food dyes, it remains advisable to monitor and perhaps moderate children's intake of artificially colored foods, especially for those who may show sensitivity to these additives. As research continues, staying informed through reliable sources and discussing any concerns with a healthcare provider is recommended to make the best choices for children's health.

Planning ADHD-Friendly Meals

Creating a meal plan isn't just about choosing the right foods; it's about ensuring they are appealing and accessible for your child throughout the day. Start with a solid breakfast that includes a good source of protein and complex carbohydrates to set the tone for the day. Snacks should be balanced and portable, like apple slices with almond butter or a small yogurt with berries. Consider incorporating a protein source, complex carbohydrates, and many colorful vegetables for main meals. Being mindful of caffeine is also important, as it can exacerbate anxiety and sleep disturbances in sensitive individuals. Some books that are currently available are, "The ADHD Diet Cookbook: Easy, Low-Sugar, High-Nutrition Recipes for Kids and Teens" by Laura Stevens and "The Kid-Friendly ADHD & Autism Cookbook, Updated and Revised: The Ultimate Guide to the Gluten-Free, Casein-Free Diet" by Pamela Compart and Dana Laake. These books include meal plans for children with ADHD and Autism.

The Importance of Physical Activity for Children with ADHD

Regular physical activity is beneficial for all children, but it can be particularly transformative for those with ADHD. Exercise isn't just about staying fit; it directly influences brain function, mood, and attention—key areas where children with ADHD might struggle. Engaging your child in regular physical activities can be a natural dose of attention-enhancing medication without side effects.

Choosing the Appropriate Activities

When choosing activities for a child with ADHD, aligning these with their interests and energy levels is crucial. This ensures they are engaged and likely to stick with the activity long-term. For instance, a child who enjoys solo tasks and has a lot of energy might thrive in individual sports like swimming or martial arts, where they can channel their energy into focused movements. In contrast, a child who enjoys social interaction and has moderate energy might find team sports like soccer or basketball fulfilling, as these provide both physical engagement and social interaction. The key is to observe what naturally interests your child and then explore physical activities that align with those interests. I completed a survey on several ADHD parent Facebook groups and found the activities most children with ADHD are involved in for stress relief are #1 swimming, #2 swimming, and #3 playing at the park. Other highly utilized activities were drawing, jumping on the trampoline, team sports, dance, and karate/jiu-jitsu-type activities. One fantastic answer was long drives in the car, looking at houses, looking for animals, etc. This parent advised it allowed for long talks that allowed her child to open up about things happening in her life. Something we don't always think of.

Structured vs. Unstructured Play

Balancing structured and unstructured play is also vital in managing ADHD symptoms effectively. Structured activities, such as martial arts or ballet, provide routine and clear expectations, which can help develop discipline and focus. These activities often involve repetitive movements and sequences that can be meditative and particularly beneficial for children who struggle with self-regulation and attention. On the other hand, unstructured play, like playing in a park or riding bikes, allows children to explore and move spontaneously. This kind of play can be incredibly beneficial for creativity and stress relief, offering them a way to burn off excess energy without the confines of strict rules or structured gameplay.

Incorporating physical activity into daily routines might seem daunting, especially for families with tight schedules or limited access to safe outdoor spaces. However, various ways to integrate more movement into everyday life doesn't necessarily require large blocks of time or special equipment. For example, short bursts of activity like jumping jacks during TV commercial breaks or dancing to favorite songs before dinner can be effective. For families living in areas with limited outdoor space, indoor obstacle courses, yoga sessions, or simple active games can keep children engaged. Even chores, when approached creatively, can become a form of physical activity; for instance, racing to see who can tidy up their room the fastest or having a dance-off while dusting. These examples may seem silly or unrealistic, which is okay. You need to think outside the box and know that short bursts of activity are just as beneficial as longer-lasting activities as long as they target your goals for your child. I feel it is important to add other activities that parents gave in my survey that they utilize that do not necessarily involve physical activity, but I think they were great ideas. Brainbreak on YouTube, Dioramas, Magna-Tiles, Diamond/Crystal painting, Plus-Plus blocks, Art for Kids Hub, Legos, sensory putty bins, slime, and Legos.

Natural Supplements for ADHD: What the Research Says

Natural supplements often emerge as a beacon of hope for many parents seeking alternatives or complements to traditional medication. Omega-3 fatty acids, zinc, magnesium, and iron, are among the most discussed in ADHD, each heralded for their unique benefits to brain health and function. Let's explore how these natural supplements might influence ADHD symptoms and what science says about their efficacy.

Omega-3 Fatty Acids

Omega-3 fatty acids, particularly EPA and DHA, are critical for brain health. They play a pivotal role in enhancing cognitive functions and managing neurodevelopmental disorders. Research suggests that children with ADHD often have lower levels of omega-3 fatty acids compared to their peers. Clinical trials have shown that supplementation can improve attention, hyperactivity, and impulsivity in children with ADHD. This is because omega-3s help regulate neurotransmitter pathways and reduce inflammation, which are crucial for a healthy brain.

Zinc

Zinc is another supplement that has shown benefits in managing ADHD symptoms. This mineral is essential for neurotransmitter function and the metabolism of melatonin, which regulates dopamine—a neurotransmitter often out of balance in ADHD. Studies have indicated that zinc supplementation can help improve attention and reduce hyperactivity and impulsivity. However, it's important to note that the efficacy of zinc can vary widely, and it is often more beneficial when used in conjunction with other treatments or dietary adjustments.

Magnesium

Magnesium, often paired with zinc in supplement regimens, plays a critical role in calming the nervous system and improving sleep quality, issues commonly faced by children with ADHD. Magnesium aids in the functioning of GABA receptors in the brain, which promote relaxation. Adequate levels of magnesium can help mitigate symptoms of restlessness and improve overall behavioral issues in children with ADHD.

Iron

Iron deficiency has also been observed in several studies of children with ADHD. Iron is crucial for dopamine synthesis and can influence the efficacy of dopamine agonists used to treat ADHD, suggesting that adequate iron levels are essential for the optimal management of ADHD symptoms. Supplementation in iron-deficient children has shown improvements in attention and learning capacities.

When considering integrating these supplements into your child's regimen, it's imperative to approach this process with caution and awareness. Supplement interactions with medications, potential side effects, and the appropriate dosages must be carefully managed. Consulting with a healthcare provider who understands the complexities of ADHD and the effects of these supplements is crucial. They can offer guidance tailored to your child's specific health needs, ensuring that any supplementation strategy is safe and effective. A healthcare provider might recommend starting with a low dose and gradually increasing it while monitoring the effects on ADHD symptoms. This careful, personalized approach ensures that the supplementation strategy is optimally tailored to your child's specific needs, maximizing potential benefits and minimizing risks.

Current Medications with Benefits and Side Effects

Navigating ADHD medications can feel like figuring out a complex map, with each route offering different challenges and rewards. It's important to remember that these medications' effectiveness and side effects can vary significantly from one child to another. This is why personalized medical care is crucial. A pediatrician or child psychiatrist will tailor the treatment to your child's specific needs. Regular follow-ups are essential to check how well the medication works and manage any side effects. Let's explore the two main types of medicines used to treat ADHD: stimulant and non-stimulant medications, each with its own benefits and potential side effects.

Stimulants

Stimulant medications, such as Methylphenidate and Amphetamines, are often the first line of treatment for ADHD. Methylphenidate, available under various brand names like Ritalin, Concerta, and Daytrana, works by increasing the levels of dopamine and norepinephrine in the brain. These neurotransmitters play critical roles in attention and behavior. Many parents report significant improvements in their child's ability to focus, maintain attention, and control impulses when taking these medications. However, the side effects can sometimes be a cause for concern. Common side effects include decreased appetite, which can lead to weight loss, difficulty sleeping, increased heart rate, and occasionally, mood swings or irritability. It's a delicate balance, managing these side effects while appreciating the benefits of enhanced focus and activity control.

Similarly, Amphetamine-based medications like Adderall, Vyvanse, and Dexedrine function by enhancing the release of neurotransmitters in the brain, thereby improving attention and reducing impulsivity. Parents often observe that their children can better concentrate on tasks, show improved academic performance, and exhibit more predictable behavior when on these medications. Yet, the side effects mirror those of Methylphenidate, with the potential for sleep disturbances, appetite suppression, and increased blood pressure. These side effects necessitate a careful, monitored approach to using stimulant medications, always considering the child's health and well-being.

The APSARD 2024 Conference reported on the development of new stimulant treatments, including a transdermal amphetamine patch and evening-dosed stimulants.

Non-Stimulants

On the other hand, non-stimulant medications provide an alternative treatment option and are sometimes used when stimulants are ineffective or cause unmanageable side effects. Atomoxetine, known by the brand name Strattera, enhances attention span and reduces impulsive behavior and hyperactivity by selectively inhibiting the reuptake of norepinephrine. However, Atomoxetine has its own set of challenges, including potential side effects like nausea, vomiting, fatigue, and, less commonly, mood swings or even suicidal thoughts. These risks require that their use be closely monitored by a healthcare professional, ensuring that the benefits outweigh the potential harms.

Guanfacine and Clonidine, marketed as Intuniv and Kapvay, respectively, are two other non-stimulant medications that target the brain's prefrontal cortex, which regulates attention, behavior, and emotions. These medications are known to aid with impulse control and hyperactivity and can be especially useful in individuals who experience side effects from or do not respond to stimulant medications. However, they, too, come with side effects such as drowsiness, fatigue, and sometimes, dry mouth and constipation. Low blood pressure and slow heart rate are potential side effects, necessitating regular monitoring.

Newer medications like viloxazine ER have shown promising results in improving symptoms and may be used in combination with stimulants for better outcomes.

The most recent research on ADHD Medications shows that both Methylphenidate (stimulant medications) and Atomoxetine (non-stimulant medications) have comparable effects of improving executive functions in people with ADHD when taken over a longer period of time. For both drugs, the best effect was on improving attention. Chronic methylphenidate improved performance on all cognitive domains. Chronic Atomoxetine improved performance on all domains except working memory. Cognitive domains include attention, inhibition, reaction time and working memory. When considering ADHD medications, the decision to medicate can be complex and deeply personal. Each child's needs are unique, and what works for one may not work for another. This decision often involves trial and error and should always be guided by a qualified healthcare provider. The goal is always to improve your child's quality of life by reducing the symptoms of ADHD with a medication plan that minimizes side effects. As a parent, your role is to provide a supportive environment that accommodates your child's needs, including fostering open communication about how they feel regarding their treatment. This supportive dialogue is essential, as it guides the adjustments in their treatment plan, ensuring it remains aligned with their evolving needs.

Cannabidiol (CBD) Gummies

The use of cannabidiol gummies for children with ADHD is an area of growing interest, but it is also one that requires careful consideration due to the limited amount of robust scientific research available. CBD is a non-psychoactive compound found in cannabis plants. Unlike THC (tetrahydrocannabinol), CBD does not produce a "high" and is often marketed for its potential therapeutic benefits, including reducing anxiety and improving focus. Research specifically focused on CBD s effects on ADHD is sparse. Most studies have been conducted on adults, with very few clinical trials involving children. Some anecdotal reports and small-scale studies suggest that CBD may help reduce anxiety and improve sleep, which can be beneficial for children with ADHD. There is also some evidence that CBD may help improve focus and reduce hyperactivity, but these findings are preliminary. The safety profile of CBD in children is not well-established. While CBD is generally considered safe for adults, children may respond differently, and there are concerns about potential side effects and interactions with other medications. The appropriate dosage of CBD for children with ADHD has not been standardized, and products can vary widely in terms of purity and concentration. Some products may contain trace amounts of THC, which can be harmful to children. CBD products are not uniformly regulated, leading to variations in quality and safety. The FDA has approved one CBD-based medication (Epidiolex) for specific types of epilepsy, but it has not approved CBD for ADHD treatment.

While there is some interest in the potential benefits of CBD for children with ADHD, the current evidence is insufficient to support its widespread use. More rigorous, large-scale studies are needed to determine its safety and efficacy. Parents considering CBD for their child's ADHD should seek guidance from healthcare professionals to make informed decisions based on the most current and reliable information. Most healthcare professionals recommend caution when considering CBD for children. Parents are advised to consult with a pediatrician or a specialist in pediatric neurology or psychiatry before starting any new treatment, including CBD.

The Role of Routine Medical Checkups

Consistent medical checkups become a cornerstone for monitoring the condition and nurturing your child's overall well-being in managing ADHD. By closely monitoring health developments, medication effects, and potential coexisting conditions, you can make informed decisions that significantly enhance your child's quality of life. During these visits, the doctor assesses the physical aspects of your child's health and the effectiveness of any ADHD medications being administered. This is crucial because the impact of these medications can vary over time as your child grows and their body changes. I cannot even tell you the number of medications my son tried. Some worked great at first, but then the benefits slowed down. Others made him lose significant weight, and he had to be taken off them. Others kept him up all night, and some he wouldn't even take because the pill was too large to swallow. It was so frustrating and often led to tears for both of us. Then, as he grew older, anxiety and depression came into play. At one point, the doctor diagnosed him with anorexia. Had the doctors not noticed his severe weight loss, I would never have known. Regular monitoring helps in tweaking dosages or making necessary changes to the medication plan, ensuring optimal effectiveness with minimal side effects. These checkups also provide an excellent opportunity to discuss any concerns you might have noticed at home or school, making them an essential part of effectively managing your child's treatment plan. Do not take these appointments lightly.

Addressing Coexisting Conditions

ADHD rarely travels alone; it often brings along companions like anxiety, depression, learning disabilities, or sleep disorders. Routine checkups are vital in identifying the coexisting conditions that might remain under the radar. Early detection and treatment of these conditions can prevent them from exacerbating ADHD symptoms, thereby smoothing the path to your child's social and academic success. For example, addressing a sleep disorder can improve attention and behavior, while managing anxiety can enhance your child's overall engagement and participation in various activities.

Nutritional Assessments

During these checkups, doctors also evaluate your child's nutritional status, which is pivotal in managing ADHD. Nutrient deficiencies, such as iron, zinc, or magnesium, can mimic or worsen ADHD symptoms, making dietary assessments integral to checkups. These evaluations ensure your child receives a balanced diet, supporting brain function and overall growth. If deficiencies are identified, healthcare providers can recommend dietary adjustments or supplements, ensuring that your child's nutritional needs are fully met to support optimal health and cognitive function.

Building a Healthcare Team

Creating a supportive healthcare team is one of the best steps you can take to manage your child's ADHD effectively. This team might include your pediatrician, a child psychiatrist, a nutritionist, and possibly an educational consultant, all working together to care for your child. Each professional brings a unique perspective, ensuring all aspects of your child's condition are addressed. This team approach improves the quality of care and gives you a robust support system, empowering you with knowledge and strategies to manage the challenges of ADHD confidently.

Chapter 12
Integrating Therapies

"It is easier to build strong children than to repair broken men."

— *Frederick Douglass*

Understanding and Choosing Behavioral Therapy

Behavioral therapy is an approach grounded not just in understanding the behaviors associated with ADHD but in actively reshaping them. This therapy isn't a one-size-fits-all solution. It is tailored to fit the unique needs and challenges of your child. The main goal of behavioral therapy is to improve your child's control over their thoughts and actions. For children with ADHD, this can mean better emotional regulation, enhanced organizational skills, and a significant reduction in disruptive behaviors. These improvements often lead to better performance in school and more stable social interactions. They also foster greater self-esteem in your child as they gain control over their impulses and actions, leading to a more empowered self-concept. The benefits extend beyond the child; as a parent, gaining practical behavioral management skills can reduce stress and increase the joy of parenting.

Types of Behavioral Therapy

Behavioral therapy for ADHD encompasses a variety of techniques, but two of the most impactful are Cognitive Behavioral Therapy (CBT) and Parent Coaching-which will be explained later. CBT focuses on changing the child's thought patterns and behaviors, contributing to emotional regulation and interpersonal interaction difficulties. It helps them identify distortions in their thinking and provides tools to change these thoughts positively, thereby influencing their behaviors. On the other hand, Behavioral Parent Coaching, described in Chapter 13, is designed for you, the parent. This training equips you with strategies to guide and manage your child's behavior effectively. You learn techniques to reinforce desirable behaviors, discourage negative behaviors, and communicate more effectively with your child. Both forms of therapy aim to create a harmonious environment that promotes positive changes in behavior.

Applied Behavioral Analysis (ABA) another option, but most often used for children with autism. It has been shown to help those with ADHD so worth mentioning. ABA is a scientific approach to understanding behavior and how it is affected by the environment. The goal is to improve socially significant behaviors through systematic interventions based on principles of learning theory. ABA techniques involve the use of reinforcement, prompting, and shaping to teach new skills and reduce problematic behaviors. Data collection and analysis are integral parts of the process to measure progress and make adjustments. It helps in teaching communication, social, academic, and life skills. ABA is also used to address a variety of behavioral issues in different settings, including schools, homes, and clinics.

Identifying the antecedents (what happens before), behaviors (the behavior itself), and consequences (what happens after) to understand the behavior's function. Developing interventions that include positive reinforcement, teaching new skills, and reducing problematic behaviors. It is important to ensure that learned behaviors transfer across different environments and situations.

What Behavioral Therapy Looks Like

Behavioral therapy typically involves regular sessions with a trained therapist who works with your child and possibly your family. During these sessions, your child might work on specific tasks to improve concentration, patience, and organizational skills. For instance, they might be asked to organize tasks, wait their turn in a conversation simulation, or identify emotions in various scenarios. It's a practical approach that addresses real-life challenges. Knowing if it's working can sometimes be as simple as noticing a smoother morning routine or less conflict over homework. More formally, improvements are often tracked through consistent feedback from you and your child's teachers and observable changes in behavior during therapy sessions.

Finding a Therapist

Choosing the right therapist is crucial. Look for professionals experienced in working with children with ADHD who come highly recommended by healthcare providers or trusted fellow parents. Key questions to ask potential therapists include their approach to behavioral therapy, success rates with children with ADHD, and philosophy regarding parent involvement. A skilled therapist should make your child feel comfortable and understood.

Integrating Therapy into Life

Integrating the techniques learned into everyday life is essential to maximize the benefits of behavioral therapy. This might mean setting up structured routines at home that mimic those used within therapy sessions, using consistent signals and rewards to encourage behavior, or even modeling emotional regulation techniques during high-stress periods of the day. Consistency between the therapy environment and home life can reinforce learning and make those positive behaviors more habitual and natural for your child.

The Potential of Art and Music Therapy

Art therapy works on a simple idea: when words are not enough, we use pictures and symbols to tell our stories. For children with ADHD who might have trouble expressing themselves with words, creating art offers a unique way to share their feelings. This kind of therapy lets your child show their emotions through activities like painting, sculpting, or drawing. Art therapy can help reduce frustration and impulsivity by providing a focused activity that calms the mind. Making art also helps your child feel a sense of accomplishment and self-worth, which are often difficult for children with ADHD. As they learn to express their emotions and experiences through art, they gain important skills for managing their feelings that help them beyond the therapy sessions, building resilience and emotional intelligence.

Music Therapy for Focus and Relaxation

Similarly, music therapy uses structured musical experiences to achieve therapeutic goals for children with ADHD. These goals might include improving focus, reducing anxiety, and enhancing social skills. Music's repetitive and predictable nature helps organize the child's thoughts and actions, making it easier for them to concentrate and stay on task. Playing an instrument or listening to certain types of music can calm their thoughts and promote relaxation. Music also provides a powerful way for children to express and connect with their feelings without relying only on words.

DIY Art and Music Activities

For days when structured therapy isn't on the schedule, having some DIY art and music activities can be an excellent way to continue the therapeutic benefits. Create a 'creativity kit' with basic art supplies like markers, clay, and paper, and let your child use these tools to create whenever they feel compelled. As said earlier in the physical activity section, many parents utilize activities like Brainbreak on YouTube, Dioramas, Magna-Tiles, Diamond/Crystal painting, Plus-Plus blocks, Art for Kids Hub, Legos, sensory putty bins, slime, and Legos.

Simple instruments like bongo drums, a ukulele, or even home-made instruments can provide an accessible way for your child to engage with music. Encourage them to write songs, make up rhythms, or even doodle to the beat of their favorite song. These activities offer spontaneous ways to reduce stress and channel energy positively, reinforcing the therapeutic goals of art and music therapy in everyday life.

Understanding Sensory Integration Therapy

Sensory integration therapy was developed to help individuals better process the sensory information they receive from their environment. For a child with ADHD, whose sensory processing system may be dysregulated, everyday sensations can be too distracting, leading to common ADHD symptoms such as inattentiveness or hyperactivity. Sensory integration therapy focuses on making sense of sensory inputs so that children can respond more appropriately in various situations, whether tolerating the touch of a clothing tag, managing the overwhelming sounds of a crowded room, or participating in activities involving complex motor skills. One doctor once explained to me that an average person can be in a room with many different noises going on and be able to hone in on who is talking to them. Children with sensory dysregulation hear all noises simultaneously at the same tone and cannot decipher what noise to listen to. The key is to provide these sensory inputs in a controlled, repetitive manner so that the child's nervous system becomes desensitized and can process them more effectively. FORBRAIN is a brain training headset your child can use at home for 10-20 minutes daily to speak, sing, or read their homework or books aloud. It helps with speech, language, and attention challenges.

Identifying Sensory Processing Issues

Recognizing sensory processing issues in children with ADHD can sometimes be challenging due to the overlap of symptoms. However, some indicators might include an unusual aversion to sensory experiences that most children find tolerable or enjoyable, such as a dislike of being touched, resistance to wearing certain clothes or being easily bothered by lights or sounds. These children might also seek intense sensory experiences, like constantly touching objects, crashing into things, or spinning frequently. Understanding these signs can help you identify whether sensory processing might be challenging for your child, guiding you toward appropriate interventions like sensory integration therapy.

Creating a Sensory-Friendly Home

Transforming your home into a sensory-friendly space can provide your child with a safe environment that minimizes sensory overload and supports their therapy goals. Start by observing your child's reactions to sensory experiences in your home environment. You might notice that certain lights are too bright or specific noises are particularly disruptive. Simple adjustments, such as using dimmable lights, adding rugs to dampen sound, or choosing soft, non-irritating fabrics for bedding and clothing, can make a significant difference. Consider creating a dedicated sensory space with a weighted blanket, stress balls, or a mini trampoline. This space can serve as a retreat for your child to regulate their senses and practice the techniques they learn in therapy.

The Role of Animal-Assisted Therapy in ADHD

When you think about therapies for ADHD, the image of a child interacting with an animal might not be the first that comes to mind. Yet, animal-assisted therapy (AAT) has emerged as a profoundly impactful method for enhancing the emotional and behavioral well-being of children with ADHD. This form of treatment involves structured interactions between a child and a trained therapy animal, typically under the guidance of a professional who tailors activities to achieve specific therapeutic outcomes. The presence of an animal in a therapeutic setting can add a layer of comfort and excitement for children, making therapy sessions more engaging and less intimidating.

Introduction to Animal-Assisted Therapy

Animal-assisted therapy encompasses a range of activities, from simply petting an animal to more structured tasks like grooming, feeding, or walking. These interactions are designed to promote improvements in physical, social, emotional, and cognitive functions. In the context of ADHD, the therapeutic goals often focus on reducing anxiety, improving attention, and enhancing social skills. Animals commonly used in this therapy include dogs, horses, cats, and even smaller pets like rabbits and guinea pigs, each offering unique interactions that cater to various therapeutic needs. Locating a reputable animal-assisted therapy program involves several considerations to ensure that it meets your child's specific needs and that the environment is safe and professionally managed. Start by seeking referrals from your child's healthcare provider or local mental health organizations. These programs should adhere to standards set by recognized organizations such as the International Association of Human-Animal Interaction Organizations (IAHAIO) or Pet Partners.

Benefits of Animal-Assisted Therapy

One of the most immediate benefits of animal-assisted therapy is the reduction in anxiety and improvement in mood it can bring. Animals have a unique way of offering unconditional acceptance, which can be incredibly comforting to a child who may struggle with self-esteem issues due to ADHD. Engaging with an animal can also be a highly mindful activity, drawing the child's full attention to the present moment, which helps manage impulsivity and improve focus. Moreover, tasks that involve caring for an animal can enhance a child's sense of responsibility and accomplishment, boosting their self-confidence. Social skills, too, are honed as children learn to take turns, follow directions, and communicate effectively during therapy sessions.

Animal-assisted therapy's structured yet flexible nature makes it highly personalized for each child's needs. For example, a child with difficulty with physical hyperactivity might benefit from walking a dog, which channels their energy into a structured activity. Conversely, a child who struggles with anxiety might find calming comfort in the steady presence of a therapy cat. This versatility makes animal-assisted therapy a valuable complement to more traditional therapeutic approaches, providing a multifaceted strategy to manage ADHD symptoms.

Manito Life Center and the Evidence-Based Equine Therapy

One specific form of outdoor therapy that has shown considerable promise for children with ADHD is equine therapy, offered at places like the Manito Life Center. Equine therapy involves structured interactions with horses, including grooming, feeding, and riding. The rhythmic, repetitive motions involved in horse riding and the need to maintain focus while riding can significantly enhance attention span, reduce impulsivity, and boost self-esteem. The horses provide non-judgmental companionship, which can be incredibly soothing for children with ADHD, who often face frequent criticism in more traditional settings. The responsibility of caring for an animal also teaches empathy and nurturing skills, which are beneficial for emotional and social development.

Animals as Companions at Home

Beyond structured therapy sessions, simply having a pet at home can contribute positively to the emotional and behavioral regulation of a child with ADHD. Pets provide consistent companionship, which can comfort a child who might feel misunderstood or isolated because of their symptoms. The daily routines of feeding, grooming, and playing with a pet can also help a child develop a sense of routine and responsibility. Furthermore, pets often provide non-verbal feedback through their behaviors and reactions, which can help children become more attuned to social cues and improve their empathy and nurturing skills.

Non-Traditional Holistic Therapies

In this section, we will explore some special ways to help your child that go beyond the usual treatments. These methods are called holistic therapies, which means they look at the whole child, not just their symptoms. We will talk about Craniosacral Therapy, a gentle treatment that helps the body feel balanced, and Nrf2 activation, a way to boost the body's natural defenses. These therapies can be used along with other treatments your child might be getting. Our goal is to give you more tools to support your child's health and happiness in a natural way.

Craniosacral Therapy (CST) for ADHD

CST is a gentle, hands-on therapy that aims to improve the functioning of the craniosacral system, which includes the membranes and cerebrospinal fluid surrounding the brain and spinal cord. Some practitioners and parents have reported benefits of CST for children with ADHD, such as improved focus, reduced hyperactivity, and enhanced overall well-being. The scientific evidence supporting CST specifically for ADHD is limited and mostly anecdotal. There are few rigorous, peer-reviewed studies validating its efficacy for ADHD. CST is considered a complementary therapy and is not universally endorsed by mainstream medical organizations as a primary treatment for ADHD. It is often used as part of a holistic approach, potentially alongside conventional treatments like behavioral therapy and medication.It is not universally recognized or regulated as a standard medical practice. Some practitioners and parents have reported benefits of CST for children with ADHD, such as improved focus, reduced hyperactivity, and enhanced overall well-being. The scientific evidence supporting CST specifically for ADHD is limited and mostly anecdotal. There are few rigorous, peer-reviewed studies validating its efficacy for

ADHD. Systematic reviews often call for more high-quality research to determine the effectiveness of CST for ADHD and other conditions. CST is typically performed by licensed healthcare professionals such as massage therapists, osteopaths, chiropractors, and physical therapists who have received specialized training in this technique.

Nrf2 (Nuclear Factor Erythroid 2-Related Factor 2) Activation for ADHD

Nrf2 is a protein that regulates the expression of antioxidant proteins and is involved in cellular defense mechanisms. The idea behind Nrf2 activation for ADHD is based on the hypothesis that oxidative stress and inflammation may play a role in the pathology of ADHD, and enhancing the body's antioxidant response could potentially alleviate some symptoms. Research on Nrf2 activation specifically for ADHD is still emerging. While there is evidence suggesting that oxidative stress may be involved in ADHD, direct studies on Nrf2 activators for ADHD are limited. Dietary approaches, such as consuming foods rich in antioxidants (e.g., fruits and vegetables high in sulforaphane), have been explored for their potential benefits, but more research is needed. Nrf2 activation is a promising area of research for various conditions, but its application for ADHD is not yet well-established or widely endorsed. Conventional treatments for ADHD, such as behavioral therapy and medications like stimulants, remain the primary recommendations by healthcare professionals.

While CST and Nrf2 activation are areas of interest for managing ADHD symptoms, they are generally considered complementary rather than primary treatments. Parents considering these therapies for their children with ADHD should do so in consultation with healthcare professionals and ensure that any alternative approaches are integrated safely with conventional treatments.

Always prioritize evidence-based therapies and consult with specialists who can provide guidance tailored to the child's specific needs.

The Impact of Outdoor Activities on ADHD

Benefits of Nature

The calming influence of natural settings is well-known, with studies showing that green spaces can significantly decrease symptoms of ADHD by improving concentration and reducing impulsiveness and hyperactivity. Nature gently engages the mind, offering sensory experiences more soothing than the harsh sensory input of city environments. Nature's sights, sounds, and textures invite easy engagement, allowing children with ADHD to focus better and feel less need for constant stimulation. The peacefulness of natural environments also helps relax their often-overworked nervous systems, reducing anxiety.

Adding nature to daily life might require some creativity for families in urban areas. Simple steps like planting a small garden on a balcony or regularly visiting local parks can make a big difference. Even indoor activities can benefit from nature; try playing nature sounds during relaxation exercises or decorating your home with plants and pictures of natural landscapes to bring the outdoors inside.

Outdoor Activities for ADHD

Activities like hiking through forest trails provide physical exercise, which is important for managing energy levels, and offer a rich sensory experience that is naturally calming. Gardening is also beneficial because it involves nurturing something from seed to bloom, teaching planning, and patience, which can be challenging for children with ADHD. Organized sports, especially those played outdoors like soccer or baseball, provide structured social interaction and regular physical activity, helping to improve self-discipline and social skills.

For many children with ADHD, the structured chaos of team sports might be overwhelming. More solitary or one-on-one sports like fishing or golf might benefit such cases. These activities still provide the benefits of outdoor engagement and physical activity in a quieter, more controlled environment. Each of these activities serves a dual purpose: they harness the therapeutic power of nature while promoting skills and behaviors that can mitigate the challenges of ADHD.

Chapter 13
Taking Care of Yourself While Caring for Your Child

"Self-care is giving the world the best of you, instead of what's left of you."

— *Katie Reed*

Navigating the complexities of ADHD can often feel like steering a ship through uncharted waters—challenging, unpredictable, and requiring constant attention. While you work hard to guide your child towards calmer seas, caring for yourself is essential without feeling guilty. This chapter aims to help you find well-deserved paths to self-care.

Building Your Support Network: Finding Community

Expanding Your Circle

The strength of a support network cannot be overstated, especially when parenting a child with ADHD. Including other parents who understand the day-to-day realities of ADHD can provide emotional solace and practical advice. Professionals such as therapists, counselors, and ADHD coaches bring expertise and strategies tailored to your child's needs. Moreover, supportive family members can offer a listening ear or a helping hand when you need respite. Each person in your network adds a layer of stability and resourcefulness, reinforcing your ability to parent at your best.

Social Media Groups

Building this network involves reaching out and connecting in various ways. With social media at an all-time high, finding groups to follow is easier than ever, and I know from experience that the support community is so worthwhile. These platforms allow for exchanging ideas and experiences to enlighten your parenting approach. Simply going into Facebook and clicking groups, then typing "ADHD Parent" in the search box will provide lists of groups on the topic. Click on them and see which ones speak to you. You can join a hundred of them if you choose—platforms like Reddit offer real-time interaction with other parents across the globe. When selecting a group, look for one that is well-moderated, active, and positive. Private groups are the best option because they are well-monitored. Sharing your experiences and learning from others in similar situations is profoundly therapeutic. It not only diminishes the feeling of isolation but also enhances your knowledge and skills in managing ADHD. Engage actively in discussions, ask questions, and offer your insights. The collective wisdom of a community can often lead to discovering new coping mechanisms and strategies that might be the perfect fit for your child's needs.

Community Resources

Your local community and the broader online community are reservoirs of resources waiting to be tapped into. Look for support groups, both in-person and online, specifically targeted towards parents of children with ADHD. These groups often host guest speakers, organize informative events, and provide a platform for sharing strategies and encouragement. Websites like CHADD (Children and Adults with Attention-Deficit/Hyperactivity Disorder) offer directories of local support groups and many online resources that can guide you in managing ADHD effectively. Local hospitals often hold support sessions on topics of children with ADHD or neurodiversity, so keep your eyes tuned to their websites, too.

Stress Management Techniques for Parents

Recognizing Signs of Stress

Navigating the day-to-day responsibilities while managing a child's ADHD can often stretch your emotional and physical resilience to its limits. Recognizing the signs of stress in yourself is the first step towards maintaining your well-being and the harmony of your entire family. Stress might manifest in various forms—perhaps you are snapping at minor annoyances, feeling perpetually tired, or struggling to sleep. These indicators are your body's signaling that it's time to step back and care for yourself.

Stress Relief Strategies

Understanding these signs, you can adopt simple yet effective stress-relief strategies that fit your busy schedule. Deep breathing exercises, for instance, are a quick and efficient way to calm your mind and can be done almost anywhere. Apps like "Calm" or "Headspace" offer guided breathing exercises and short meditations that fit into a tight schedule—often taking no more than three minutes. YouTube also offers many free versions of three-minute meditations. These small pockets of mindfulness can significantly decrease stress levels and increase your capacity to handle parenting challenges more gracefully.

Short Periods of Self-Care

Engaging in self-care doesn't require grand gestures or elaborate plans. Consider integrating short walks into your routine, perhaps during a lunch break or while your child is at a playdate. These brief moments of physical activity can significantly elevate your mood and clear your mind, offering a fresh perspective on daily challenges. Similarly, carving out time for reading—even if it's just a few pages each day before bed—can be a peaceful retreat from the day's demands, allowing you to escape into different worlds and perspectives.

Find Your Stress Reliever

Another enriching self-care practice is engaging in a hobby that resonates with your interests. You can paint, garden, knit, golf, or play an instrument. These activities nurture your spirit and model the importance of personal interests and lifelong learning for your child.

The Importance of Parental Self-Care: Guilt-Free Practices

Amid managing schedules, appointments, and the unique challenges that come with raising a child with ADHD, taking time for yourself might sometimes feel like a luxury you can't afford. The phrase "self-care" often carries an unjust stigma of selfishness, especially among parents deeply committed to their children's well-being. However, reframing self-care as a vital component of effective parenting is crucial. It's not about indulging at the expense of your child's needs; it's about replenishing your energy and maintaining your health so you can be the parent your child deserves. Just as you're instructed to put on your oxygen mask first in an airplane emergency, ensuring your well-being is essential for fully caring for others.

Create Self-Care Routines

Creating a sustainable self-care routine involves regular self-reflection and commitment. Start by identifying times in your weekly schedule that consistently work best for self-care activities. Early mornings, lunch hours, or evenings offer pocket time dedicated to your well-being. Establishing a routine helps in making self-care a habit rather than an afterthought. Incorporate a mix of physical, emotional, and spiritual practices that address different aspects of your well-being. Depending on your personal beliefs and preferences, this might include yoga, meditation, journaling, or attending religious services. The key is consistency and intentionality, ensuring that these activities are not squeezed into your schedule but are a fundamental part.

You Deserve This Time

Overcoming feelings of guilt associated with taking time for self-care is often one of the biggest hurdles for parents. Guilt can stem from an internalized belief that good parenting means constant self-sacrifice. However, it's important to challenge this notion and recognize that neglecting your needs can lead to burnout, resentment, and decreased parenting effectiveness. Remind yourself that self-care is an act of self-preservation, not selfishness. Over time, as you experience the benefits of regular self-care, guilt will likely diminish, replaced by an understanding of its importance in your family's overall health and happiness.

By cultivating these habits, you enhance your quality of life and set a powerful example for your child. Demonstrating the importance of personal well-being teaches children to value and care for themselves, a lesson that will serve them well throughout their lives. So, as you navigate the complexities of parenting, remember that caring for yourself is not just beneficial—it's essential.

Balancing Work and Parenting: Strategies for Success

Achieving a balance between your professional responsibilities and parenting a child with ADHD can sometimes feel like you're being pulled in two opposite directions. Each role demands your attention, energy, and time—resources that are not always available. The key to managing this balance is not to aim for a perfect equilibrium but to create a flexible framework that allows you to shift your focus without losing sight of your priorities.

Work-Life Integration

In today's dynamic work environment, integrating work and life responsibilities can often be more practical than balancing them as separate entities. Flexible work arrangements can be a game-changer in this aspect. Consider negotiating with your employer for flexible hours or working from home on certain days if your job allows. This flexibility can make a significant difference, allowing you to be present for your child during crucial times, such as homework or therapy sessions, while still meeting your work obligations. Additionally, explore the use of technology to streamline your tasks. Tools like cloud-based document sharing, project management apps, and virtual meeting platforms can increase your efficiency, enabling you to manage work tasks more swiftly and effectively.

In both work and home settings, prioritize tasks based on their importance and deadlines. Learn to differentiate between what must be done and what can wait. This prioritization can help reduce the feeling of being overwhelmed and ensure that you focus your energy where it's most needed. At home, involve your family in household responsibilities. Delegating tasks to your partner or children can teach them valuable skills and lighten your load. Make a list of weekly chores and assign them based on age and ability; this helps manage the household more efficiently and fosters teamwork and responsibility.

Apply similar principles in your work. Delegate tasks when possible, and don't hesitate to collaborate with colleagues on big projects. It is very common for parents with children with ADHD to overwork themselves because that is one area of their lives they can control. Do not fall into that rabbit hole. Understanding that you don't have to manage everything alone can alleviate great stress and increase your productivity as a parent and a professional.

Time Management Tips

Effective time management is essential for juggling work and parenting responsibilities. Start by identifying your high-energy periods during the day and aligning your most demanding professional and parental tasks to these times. For example, if you are a morning person, you might schedule essential work tasks and your child's most challenging homework sessions during these hours. Utilizing tools such as digital calendars can help you track work deadlines and family commitments, ensuring nothing important slips through the cracks.

Batch processing similar tasks can save you significant time and energy. Group similar work tasks together and do the same for household chores. This method reduces the time spent switching between different tasks, which can affect productivity. Additionally, setting clear start and end times for work can help you avoid the pitfall of overworking, ensuring you have dedicated time to spend with your family without work distractions.

Communication with Employers

Open and honest communication with your employer about your family's needs is crucial. Discuss these needs with your employer if you require accommodations to support your parenting responsibilities, such as leaving early for doctor's appointments or attending school meetings. When you approach these conversations, come prepared with suggestions for how you will manage your responsibilities and maintain your performance. For instance, if you need to leave early, offer to complete tasks before you leave or make up the time later. Being proactive about solutions can make these discussions more productive and show your employer you are committed to your role.

It's also beneficial to educate your employer about ADHD if your child's needs might impact your work life. Providing them with basic information about the challenges and requirements of parenting a child with ADHD can foster understanding and support from your workplace.

Seeking Professional Help: Therapy for Parents and Families

Recognizing when to seek professional help is a pivotal step for any parent, especially when navigating the added complexities of ADHD within the family. It's vital to understand that reaching out for help is not a sign of failure but rather an act of strength and commitment to your family's well-being. The indicators that professional intervention might be beneficial can vary. Still, they often involve persistent feelings of stress, anxiety, or strain in family relationships that do not seem to improve despite your best efforts. You might find that emotional outbursts are more frequent, conflicts are more challenging to resolve, or that the stress of managing ADHD is impacting your health and happiness. These signs suggest that professional therapy's structured support could benefit your challenges.

What Therapy is Right For Your Family

Therapy comes in several forms, each serving unique needs. Individual therapy can provide a confidential space to address personal challenges and develop coping strategies. It often focuses on enhancing personal resilience and managing stress or anxiety directly associated with parenting challenges. On the other hand, family therapy involves multiple family members and focuses on improving communication, resolving conflicts, and fostering a better understanding among family members. This type of therapy is particularly beneficial in addressing the dynamics that ADHD can create within a family, helping all members learn strategies to support each other effectively.

Support Groups

Support groups represent another form of therapeutic engagement, offering peer support and professional guidance. These groups are typically led by a therapist or experienced facilitator, allowing you to share your experiences and learn from others facing similar challenges. The collective wisdom and communal sense of understanding found in support groups can be incredibly comforting and enlightening. Moreover, these groups often introduce practical strategies and resources for managing ADHD in family settings.

Why Should You Incorporate Professionals

The benefits of seeking professional support are extensive. Therapy can provide you with tailored coping strategies that are effective in managing the unique challenges posed by ADHD. It offers emotional support from professionals who understand the complexities of ADHD and can validate your experiences and feelings. This professional guidance can be instrumental in navigating your child's ADHD, offering fresh perspectives and evidence-based strategies that enhance your ability to support your child's development and well-being. Behavioral Parent Coaching is a game changer for most parents and something you should consider if you are struggling.

The Role of Behavioral Parent Coaching in ADHD Management

Navigating parenting when your child has ADHD requires more than just love and patience; it needs specific strategies and insights tailored to your unique challenges. This is where parent coaching comes in. Unlike traditional therapy or counseling, parent coaching is a practical, action-oriented service that focuses on improving your parenting skills. It offers specialized support to help you handle the unique needs of your child with ADHD.

What is Behavioral Parent Coaching

Parent coaching is anchored in the present and the practical. It involves working with a coach who understands the complexities of ADHD and its impact on family dynamics. This coach provides personalized guidance, helping you develop specific strategies to manage daily challenges, improve communication with your child, and implement effective behavioral interventions. The goal is to empower you with the tools and confidence needed to handle the nuances of ADHD parenting more effectively.

The benefits of engaging with a parent coach are numerous:

1. It enhances your parenting skills by providing tailored strategies that address your child's needs. This specialized approach helps you more effectively manage common ADHD-related issues such as impulsivity, inattention, and hyperactivity.
2. Parent coaching can significantly alleviate parental stress by offering reliable support and practical solutions that make day-to-day management smoother. This stress reduction can lead to a more harmonious home environment and positively affect your relationship with your child.

3. Parent coaching aims to strengthen family dynamics. It equips all family members with the understanding and tools needed to interact more positively, fostering a supportive environment conducive to everyone's growth and well-being.

What to Expect With Behavioral Parent Coaching

When working with a parent coach, you can expect a collaborative relationship where your family's needs and values are prioritized. Initially, the coach will likely conduct an assessment to understand your specific challenges. Following this, goals are set collaboratively, ensuring they align with your child's expectations and the desired outcomes. During regular sessions, you will learn new strategies and techniques, which you will then be encouraged to implement. The coach provides ongoing feedback and support, helping you fine-tune these strategies to ensure they are as effective as possible. This process enables you to make sustained progress toward your goals.

In engaging a parent coach, you are taking a proactive step towards not just managing your child's ADHD but also enhancing your family's overall quality of life. This supportive partnership can transform how you navigate ADHD, turning challenges into opportunities for growth and learning. As you continue to apply the insights and strategies from your coaching sessions, you will likely find that you are not just surviving the world of ADHD parenting but thriving in it.

Chapter 14
Embracing ADHD

"The best way to predict the future is to create it."

— *Peter Drucker*

This new day in your journey with ADHD is about embracing and celebrating every aspect of this unique neurodiversity. It's about turning what might seem like insurmountable challenges into remarkable strengths. Imagine, for a moment, the incredible energy, creativity, and potential within ADHD, characteristics that have propelled countless individuals toward astonishing achievements. This chapter is dedicated to transforming the narrative surrounding ADHD from struggle to success and empowerment.

Celebrating ADHD Success Stories

Numerous individuals with ADHD have not only succeeded but have reshaped the world in their unique ways. Their stories are not just tales of overcoming but are powerful testaments to the potential that ADHD holds. Take, for example, the story of a well-known entrepreneur whose relentless energy and ability to think outside the box helped him create some of the most enduring technological innovations—yes, the founder of a major computer company had ADHD. His ability to hyper-focus on his passions led to technological advancements that changed how the world communicates, works, and entertains. These stories are essential for their inspiration and how they shift our understanding of ADHD from a deficit to a difference. Many well-known individuals have been diagnosed with ADHD, showcasing that it is possible to achieve great success despite the challenges associated with the condition. Here are ten famous people who have been reported to have ADHD:

1. Michael Phelps - Olympic swimmer and the most decorated Olympian of all time.
2. Simone Biles - Olympic gymnast and multiple gold medalist.

3. Justin Timberlake - Singer, songwriter, actor, and record producer.
4. Will Smith - Actor, rapper, and film producer.
5. Emma Watson - Actress and activist known for her role as Hermione Granger in the "Harry Potter" series.
6. Jim Carrey - Comedian and actor known for his energetic and expressive performances.
7. Solange Knowles - Singer, songwriter, and younger sister of Beyoncé.
8. Channing Tatum - Actor, producer, and dancer known for roles in films like "Magic Mike" and "21 Jump Street."
9. Howie Mandel - Comedian, actor, and television host.
10. Ty Pennington - Television host and carpenter known for his role on "Extreme Makeover: Home Edition."

These individuals have not only managed their ADHD but have also excelled in their respective fields, serving as inspirations to many who live with the condition.

Imagine transforming ADHD's unique challenges into strengths. This isn't just about adapting to the neurotypical world; it's about reshaping that world to recognize and celebrate neurodiversity. For instance, a child's impulsivity, often viewed negatively, can be channeled into a remarkable ability to think quickly and act bravely in situations requiring rapid decision-making. Their seemingly boundless energy can be directed into creativity and innovation, turning a simple school project into an extraordinary exploration of new ideas.

Promoting a Culture of Celebration

In this light, it becomes essential to cultivate an environment where every victory, no matter the size, is celebrated. This practice builds resilience and confidence, teaching children with ADHD—

and their families—to recognize and value their progress. Establishing a routine, such as a weekly family celebration night, can provide regular acknowledgment and reinforcement of positive behaviors and achievements. During these celebrations, focus on the effort and growth rather than just the outcome. Discuss what was learned and how challenges were navigated. This enhances self-esteem and instills a mindset that views challenges as opportunities to learn and grow.

As you move forward, let each day celebrate the unique and extraordinary aspects of ADHD. Let it remind you of the creativity, resilience, and boundless potential that lies within this condition. With each story shared and each success celebrated, you are not only reshaping the narrative of ADHD but also actively contributing to a more inclusive and understanding world.

Support the ADHD Community

As you approach the end of this guide, please reflect on the value this book has given you. This book was crafted as a resource and a companion on your path to understanding and managing ADHD in your family. If you've found value in the strategies, stories, and support offered here, consider the impact your insights could have on others navigating similar paths.

Think about the early days of your journey, filled with uncertainties and the thirst for understanding that led you to seek out resources like this one. Imagine another parent in the same situation you once were—searching for answers, guidance, and reassurance. By sharing your thoughts on this book, you contribute more than just a review; your review serves as valuable advice to fellow parents and supports the broader mission of reshaping the conversation around ADHD.

I invite you to share your review. Your voice matters, whether detailed feedback, a quick note of thanks, or constructive suggestions. It's more than just a review; it's part of a more significant effort to empower parents and caregivers, providing them with the resources they need to help their children thrive in every stage of life. As you write, remember the impact your words can have, offering another parent the same hope and guidance that perhaps this book once provided you.

https://amzn.to/3XeYwEO

Conclusion

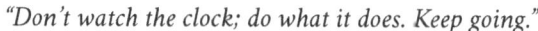

"Don't watch the clock; do what it does. Keep going."

— *Sam Levenson*

As we reach the end of this journey together, I want you to reflect on the transformative path that parenting a child with ADHD entails. It's a road marked by challenges but also rich with opportunities for growth, deeper understanding, and immense joy. From the moment of diagnosis to navigating daily triumphs and trials, this journey reshapes our world in unexpected and rewarding ways.

Throughout this book, we've examined many strategies and ideas. We've learned about ADHD, how it works in the brain, and how it shows up at different ages. We've discussed useful parenting tips that focus on helping kids control their emotions, make friends, and get the support they need in school. We've also discussed how important it is to make good lifestyle choices, like eating healthy and staying active, to help manage ADHD.

We've talked about how ADHD isn't just a set of challenges but a unique way of seeing the world, full of notable strengths and abilities. By looking at ADHD this way, we see our children's value and skills and find new opportunities we might have missed.

Your role as an advocate for your child is vital. Whether at school or in the community, your support helps people understand and accept ADHD. With an upbeat, strength-focused approach to parenting, you become a key person in your child's life, helping them use their unique abilities and face challenges.

We must also care for ourselves while we work to support our children. Self-care is not a luxury; it is essential. It keeps us strong and ready to help our children. Remember, taking care of yourself is also taking care of your child.

Now, take these strategies and insights into your daily life. Reach out to support networks, connect with other parents who understand your challenges and successes, and seek professional help when needed. You are not alone; a supportive community is on your journey.

Thank you for sharing this journey with me. We can guide our children toward thriving futures with persistence, love, and suitable approaches. Keep moving forward with hope and resilience; every small step you take is a leap toward a brighter tomorrow for you and your child.

If you would like to explore more of my published books, click/scan the links below:

 https://bit.ly/3ZgvTcW

If you would like to access FREE parenting charts and resources to implement strategies IMMEDIATELY click/scan here

http://bit.ly/3AvAkX0

References

- ADDA. (n.d.). *Support groups for adults.* ADDA. https://add.org/adhd-support-groups/
- ADDitude. (n.d.). *ACT: Therapy that's uniquely useful to an ADHD brain.* ADDitude. https://www.additudemag.com/act-therapy-acceptance-commitment-adhd/
- ADDitude. (n.d.). *ADHD and reading comprehension: 11 strategies for success.* ADDitude. https://www.additudemag.com/adhd-reading-comprehension/
- ADDitude. (n.d.). *ADHD essay writing help: 18 strategies for better school performance.* ADDitude. https://www.additudemag.com/write-well/
- ADDitude. (n.d.). *ADHD myths & fallacies - Debunked: The truth about ADD.* ADDitude Magazine. https://www.additudemag.com/adhd-myths-and-facts-learn-the-truth-about-attention-deficit/
- ADDitude. (n.d.). *ADHD success stories: Students & parents share their tips.* ADDitude. https://www.additudemag.com/will-our-kids-be-ok/
- ADDitude. (n.d.). *Art therapy: Alternative treatment for ADHD symptoms.* ADDitude. https://www.additudemag.com/treatment/art-therapy/.
- ADDitude. (n.d.). *Behavior therapy for ADHD: How to find a therapist.* ADDitude. https://www.additudemag.com/behavior-therapy-how-to-find-a-therapist-adhd/
- ADDitude. (n.d.). *Choosing a doctor for ADHD diagnosis and treatment.* ADDitude. https://www.additudemag.com/choosing-a-doctor-for-treatment/
- ADDitude. (n.d.). *Distance learning tools: Educational apps for ADHD.* ADDitude. https://www.additudemag.com/educational-apps-distance-learning-adhd-2020/
- ADDitude. (n.d.). *Easy dinner ideas: Meal planning for ADHD families.* ADDitude. https://www.additudemag.com/category/manage-adhd-life/home-organization/meal-planning/
- ADDitude. (n.d.). *Executive function skills & ADHD: Goal setting for students.* ADDitude. https://www.additudemag.com/executive-function-skills-adhd-goal-setting/
- ADDitude. (n.d.). *"How can I prepare my ADHD teen for 9th grade?"* ADDitude. https://www.additudemag.com/9th-grade-adhd-student-preparing-for-high-school/
- ADDitude. (n.d.). *How to advocate for your child with ADHD.* ADDitude.

https://www.additudemag.com/how-to-advocate-for-your-child-guide-for-adhd-parents/

- ADDitude. (n.d.). How to improve social skills in children with ADHD. ADDitude. https://www.additudemag.com/how-to-improve-social-skills-adhd-children/
- ADDitude. (n.d.). Living with ADHD: 80 coping strategies for ADD. ADDitude. https://www.additudemag.com/dealing-with-adhd-80-coping-strategies/
- ADDitude. (n.d.). Managing transitions for children with ADHD. ADDitude. https://www.additudemag.com/managing-transitions-adhd-children/
- ADDitude. (n.d.). Middle school issues: Challenges kids with ADHD will face. ADDitude. https://www.additudemag.com/slideshows/middle-school-issues-challenges-adhd-students/
- ADDitude. (n.d.). Organization tips for home: Clutter, money, meals & more. ADDitude. https://www.additudemag.com/category/manage-adhd-life/home-organization/
- ADDitude. (n.d.). Positive parenting styles: Build self-esteem & more. ADDitude. https://www.additudemag.com/category/parenting-adhd-kids/positive-parenting/
- ADDitude. (n.d.). Sibling relationships and ADHD. ADDitude. https://www.additudemag.com/sibling-relationships-adhd-families/
- ADDitude. (n.d.). Social skills for kids with ADHD. ADDitude Magazine. https://www.additudemag.com/social-skills-for-kids-friendships-adhd/
- ADHD Centre. (n.d.). Children with ADHD and routines: Building healthy structures. ADHD Centre. https://www.adhdcentre.co.uk/children-with-adhd-and-routines/
- Baer, Donald M., Montrose M. Wolf, and Todd R. Risley. "Some Current Dimensions of Applied Behavior Analysis." Journal of Applied Behavior Analysis, vol. 1, no. 1, 1968, pp. 91-97.
- Bain Health and Wellness Center. (n.d.). Collaboration. Bain Health and Wellness Center. https://bainhwc.com/collaboration
- Base Articles. (n.d.). The art of self-care: Prioritizing your wellbeing in a hectic world. Base Articles. https://basearticles.com/the-art-of-self-care-prioritizing-your-wellbeing-in-a-hectic-world.html
- Beyond BookSmart. (n.d.). ADHD and emotional dysregulation: Signs & how to improve. Beyond BookSmart. https://www.beyondbooksmart.com/executive-functioning-strategies-blog/adhd-emotional-dysregulation
- Bolduc, J., & Guay, K. (2021). Rhythmic training: An innovative approach to remediation of phonological dyslexia. The Canadian Music Educator, 62(3), 7-10.
- Brain Balance Centers. (n.d.). The benefits of exercise for children with ADHD.

Brain Balance Centers. https://www.brainbalancecenters.com/blog/exercise-children-adhd

- Bryan, Nathan S., et al. "Nrf2 Activation: A Potential Strategy for Preventing Cardiovascular Disease." Oxidative Medicine and Cellular Longevity, vol. 2013, Article ID 586507, 2013, https://www.hindawi.com/journals/omcl/2013/586507/. Accessed 16 June 2024.

- Caregivers in Canada. (n.d.). Self-care strategies: Prioritizing wellness in the caregiving profession with Maria. Caregivers in Canada. https://caregiversin-canada.com/self-care-strategies/

- Centers for Disease Control and Prevention. (n.d.). ADHD in the classroom. CDC. https://www.cdc.gov/ncbddd/adhd/school-success.html

- Centers for Disease Control and Prevention. (n.d.). Parent training in behavior management for ADHD. CDC. https://www.cdc.gov/ncbddd/adhd/behavior-therapy.html

- CHADD. (n.d.). Early ADHD treatment prevents serious complications. CHADD ADHD Weekly. https://chadd.org/adhd-weekly/early-adhd-treatment-prevents-serious-complications/

- CHADD. (n.d.). 5 effective positive reinforcement tips for your child with ADHD. CHADD ADHD Weekly. https://chadd.org/adhd-weekly/5-effective-positive-reinforcement-tips-for-your-child-with-adhd/

- CHADD. (n.d.). Homework help for ADHD. CHADD. https://chadd.org/for-parents/homework-help-for-adhd/

- CHADD. (n.d.). Parenting a child with ADHD. CHADD. https://chadd.org/for-parents/overview/

- Cleveland Clinic. (n.d.). Caregiver burnout: What it is, symptoms & prevention. Cleveland Clinic. https://my.clevelandclinic.org/health/diseases/9225-caregiver-burnout

- Commission 2021. (n.d.). Alternative therapies for managing ADHD. Commission 2021. https://comission2021.com/21092-alternative-therapies-for-managing-adhd-21/

- Comprehension: Defining the Key to Understanding | Voyager Sopris Learning. https://www.voyagersopris.com/vsl/blog/comprehension-defining-the-key-to-understanding

- Cortese, Samuele. "Cannabis and Cannabinoids for ADHD: Hype or Hope?" Lancet Psychiatry, vol. 7, no. 12, 2020, pp. 971-972.

- Deep End Talent Strategies. (n.d.). Sleep for well-being and productivity. Retrieved from https://www.deependstrategies.com/our-blog/sleep-for-well-being-and-productivity

- Exploring Online Homeschooling for Middle School: A Comprehensive Guide - Legacy Online School. https://legacyonlineschool.com/blog/online-homeschooling-for-middle-school-2.html

- Faminic. (2023). *Using natural consequences in discipline: The ultimate guide to positive parenting*. Faminic. https://faminic.com/natural-consequences/
- Forbrain. (n.d.). *30 fun and engaging ADHD activities for kids*. Forbrain. https://www.forbrain.com/adhd-learning/adhd-activities-for-kids/
- Gadjetguru.com. (2023, December 6). *Mood swings and ADHD and emotional regulation: Coping techniques*. Gadjetguru.com. https://www.gadjetguru.com/2023/12/06/mood-swings-and-adhd-and-emotional-regulation-coping-techniques/
- Giddings, V. L. (2023). *Meeting Free Appropriate Public Education and Least Restrictive Environment Requirements for Students With Disabilities During the Coronavirus-19 Pandemic: Implications for Special Education Directors.* https://core.ac.uk/download/580029903.pdf
- Gray, Joshua M., et al. "Cannabidiol (CBD) and its potential therapeutic use for ADHD." *Journal of Pediatric Neurology*, vol. 16, no. 2, 2018, pp. 127-134.
- Greater Good Science Center. (n.d.). *How four deep breaths can help kids calm down*. Greater Good. https://greatergood.berkeley.edu/article/item/how_four_deep_breaths_can_help_kids_calm_down
- Greater Good Science Center. (n.d.). *Seven ways to foster empathy in kids*. Greater Good Magazine. https://greatergood.berkeley.edu/article/item/seven_ways_to_foster_empathy_in_kids
- Harkins, J. (n.d.). *Mindfulness for ADHD: Benefits and activities for kids*. He's Extraordinary. https://hes-extraordinary.com/manage-adhd-mindfulness
- Hartman, Steven E., and Louis C. Norton. "Craniosacral Therapy Is Not Medicine." *Physical Therapy* vol. 82, no. 11, 2002, pp. 1146-1147.
- Health for Life. (n.d.). *How to cope with ADHD and how counseling can help*. Health for Life. https://healthforlifegr.com/how-to-cope-with-adhd-and-how-counseling-can-help/
- Healthline. (n.d.). *ADHD rating scale: What it is and how to understand it*. Healthline. https://www.healthline.com/health/adhd/rating-scale.
- Healthline. (n.d.). *Breaking down the stigma surrounding ADHD*. Healthline. https://www.healthline.com/health/adhd/stigma
- HealthyChildren.org. (n.d.). *Diagnosing ADHD in children: Guidelines & information for parents*. HealthyChildren.org. https://www.healthychildren.org/English/health-issues/conditions/adhd/Pages/Diagnosing-ADHD-in-Children-Guidelines-Information-for-Parents.aspx
- HelpGuide.org. (n.d.). *ADHD parenting tips*. HelpGuide.org. https://www.helpguide.org/articles/add-adhd/when-your-child-has-attention-deficit-disorder-adhd.htm

- How To Manage Your Family Life and Home Activities - News Health - Link Sharing Sites. https://linksharingsites.com/2020/06/14/how-to-manage-your-family-life-and-home-activities-news-health/
- IamPsychiatry. (n.d.). Adult ADHD medication titration. Retrieved from https://www.iampsychiatry.com/adult-adhd-medication
- Isfandnia, F., Masri, S. E., Radua, J., & Rubia, K. (2024). The Effects of Chronic administration of stimulant and non-stimulant medications on executive Functions in ADHD: A Systematic Review and Meta-Analysis. Neuroscience & Biobehavioral Reviews/Neuroscience and Biobehavioral Reviews, 105703. https://doi.org/10.1016/j.neubiorev.2024.105703
- JMD Hindi. (n.d.). The joyful companionship of pets: A treasure for humanity. JMD Hindi. https://jmdhindi.com/the-joyful-companionship-of-pets-a-treasure-for-humanity/
- Johns Hopkins University. (n.d.). Recent trends in stimulant medication use among U.S. children. Retrieved from https://pure.johnshopkins.edu/en/publications/recent-trends-in-stimulant-medication-use-among-us-children-4
- Juno Counseling. (n.d.). The power of sensory rooms for autism and ADHD. Juno Counseling. https://www.junocounseling.com/post/creating-calm-and-comfort-the-power-of-sensory-rooms-for-autism-and-adhd
- Kensler, Thomas W., et al. "Nrf2: A Master Regulator of Detoxification and Cytoprotection." Molecular Carcinogenesis, vol. 42, no. 1, 2003, pp. 13-19.
- Lancia, G., PhD. (2024, March 13). Social skills training for kids: Top resources for teachers. PositivePsychology.com. https://positivepsychology.com/social-skills-for-kids/
- Leaf, Ronald, et al. A Work in Progress: Behavior Management Strategies and a Curriculum for Intensive Behavioral Treatment of Autism. DRL Books, 1999.
- Link Sharing Sites. (2020, June 14). How to manage your family life and home activities. News Health. https://linksharingsites.com/2020/06/14/how-to-manage-your-family-life-and-home-activities-news-health/
- Luna Respite and Learning. (n.d.). Sensory-friendly workouts: Supporting sensory processing in children with special needs. Retrieved from https://www.lunarespiteandlearning.com/post/sensory-friendly-workouts-supporting-sensory-processing-in-children-with-special-needs
- Mastering Productivity: Unleash the Power of Pomodoro Technique Apps. https://oddnoodle.com/pomodoro-technique-apps/
- Mattingly, G., MD. (2024, January 26). Late breaking news from APSARD 2024 Conference. Psychiatric Times. https://www.psychiatrictimes.com/view/late-breaking-news-from-apsard-2024-conference
- Mayo Clinic. (n.d.). Attention-deficit/hyperactivity disorder (ADHD) in children. Mayo Clinic. https://www.mayoclinic.org/diseases-conditions/adhd/symptoms-causes/syc-20350889

- *Mendonça Alves, L., Correa Celeste, L., Reis, C., Lalain, M., & Ghio, A. (2013). The perception of fluency in the reading aloud of dyslexic children and regular readers.*
- *Nampa Imagine. (n.d.). 5 ways to cope with anxiety as a teen. Nampa Imagine. https://www.nampaimagine.com/mental-health-blog/ways-to-cope-with-anxiety-as-a-teen/*
- *National Center for Biotechnology Information. (n.d.). Emotional dysregulation in children with attention-deficit/hyperactivity disorder (ADHD). PubMed Central (PMC). https://www.ncbi.nlm.nih.gov/pmc/articles/PMC5110580/*
- *National Center for Biotechnology Information. (n.d.). Music therapy for attention deficit hyperactivity disorder (ADHD). PubMed Central (PMC). https://www.ncbi.nlm.nih.gov/pmc/articles/PMC6481398/*
- *National Center for Biotechnology Information. (n.d.). Parent emotion expression and autonomic-linked emotion regulation in children with and without ADHD. PubMed Central (PMC). https://www.ncbi.nlm.nih.-gov/pmc/articles/PMC8315005/*
- *National Center for Biotechnology Information. (n.d.). Social skills training for attention deficit hyperactivity disorder (ADHD). PubMed Central (PMC). https://www.ncbi.nlm.nih.gov/pmc/articles/PMC6587063/*
- *National Center for Biotechnology Information. (n.d.). The neurobiological basis of ADHD. PubMed Central (PMC). https://www.ncbi.nlm.nih.gov/pmc/articles/PMC3016271/.*
- *National Center for Complementary and Integrative Health (NCCIH). "Craniosacral Therapy." NCCIH, U.S. Department of Health and Human Services, https://nccih.nih.gov/health/craniosacral. Accessed 16 June 2024.*
- *National Center for Learning Disabilities. (n.d.). Parent Advocacy Resources. Retrieved from https://www.ncld.org/what-we-do/advocacy/*
- *N2y. (n.d.). Understanding the differences between an IEP and a 504 plan. n2y. https://www.n2y.com/blog/iep-vs-504-plan/.*
- *National Institute on Drug Abuse. "Is Marijuana Safe and Effective as Medicine?" NIDA for Teens, https://teens.drugabuse.gov/drug-facts/marijuana-medicine. Accessed 16 June 2024.*
- *Non-Perfect Parenting. (n.d.). Introducing chores to children: A practical guide for parents. Non-Perfect Parenting. https://nonperfectparenting.-com/introducing-chores-to-children/*
- *NYU Langone Health. (n.d.). PEERS social skills program. NYU Langone Health. https://nyulangone.org/locations/child-study-center/peers-social-skills-program*
- *Nutrition for ADHD & Brain Health. https://somaandsoul.ca/blog/understanding-the-role-of-nutrition-in-adhd-brain-health/*

- O'Brien, E. (2024, March 1). ADHD Research Roundup: March 1, 2024. Psychiatric Times. https://www.psychiatrictimes.com/view/adhd-research-roundup-march-1-2024
- Psych Central. (n.d.). How cognitive behavioral therapy can help with ADHD. Psych Central. https://psychcentral.com/adhd/cognitive-behavioral-therapy-for-adhd
- Psychiatric Times, (2024, March 1). ADHD Research Roundup: New genes linked to ADHD identified, potentially paving the way for new treatments. www.psychiatrictimes.com/view/adhd-research-roundup-march-1-2024.
- Rofiah, N. H. (n.d.). Identifying children with dyslexia in the classroom. Retrieved from https://core.ac.uk/download/83526096.pdf
- Sachs Center. (n.d.). Why children with ADHD need to play more. https://sachscenter.com/why-children-with-adhd-need-to-play-more/
- Science Daily. (2023, February 23). Researchers link 27 genetic variants to ADHD. https://www.sciencedaily.com/releases/2023/02/230209114741.htm
- Second Step. (n.d.). Social-emotional learning for PreK-12. Second Step. https://www.secondstep.org/
- Semel Institute for Neuroscience and Human Behavior. (n.d.). PEERS. Semel Institute for Neuroscience and Human Behavior. https://www.semel.ucla.edu/peers
- Soma & Soul. (n.d.). Nutrition for ADHD & brain health. Retrieved from https://somaandsoul.ca/blog/understanding-the-role-of-nutrition-in-adhd-brain-health/
- Sleep Foundation. (n.d.). ADHD and sleep problems: How are they related? Sleep Foundation. https://www.sleepfoundation.org/mental-health/adhd-and-sleep
- Tenenbaum, L. S. (2012). A School-Based Intervention for Third Grade Students Experiencing Test Anxiety. https://doi.org/10.57709/2326608
- The Childhood Collective. (2021, October 14). Teach growth mindset to your child with ADHD (or any child). The Childhood Collective. https://thechildhoodcollective.com/2021/10/14/4-strategies-to-teach-growth-mindset-to-your-child-with-adhd-or-any-child/
- The Kid-Friendly ADHD & Autism Cookbook, Updated and Revised: The Ultimate Guide to the Gluten-Free, Casein-Free Diet - NutriScape.Net. https://www.nutriscape.net/the-kid-friendly-adhd-autism-cookbook-updated-and-revised-the-ultimate-guide-to-the-gluten-free-casein-free-diet/
- 360 Counseling, LLC. (n.d.). Embracing healing: A guide to mental health therapy. 360 Counseling, LLC. https://clearwater360counseling.com/a-guide-to-mental-health-therapy/
- Today's Parent. (n.d.). 5 tips for helping your kid with ADHD have better playdates. Today's Parent. https://www.todaysparent.com/family/special-needs/tips-for-helping-your-kid-with-adhd-have-better-playdates/

- Total Care ABA. (n.d.). *How dozens of genes may contribute to autism?* Retrieved from https://www.totalcareaba.com/autism/how-dozens-of-genes-may-contribute-to-autism
- Training & Technical Assistance Center (T/TAC) at William & Mary. (n.d.). *Classroom interventions for attention deficit/hyperactivity disorder. The College of William & Mary.* https://education.wm.edu/centers/ttac/documents/packets/adhd.pdf
- Understood.org. (n.d.). *7 discipline tips when your child has ADHD. Understood.org.* https://www.understood.org/en/articles/adhd-discipline-strategies
- University of the People. (n.d.). *8 successful people with ADHD you should know about. University of the People.* https://www.uopeople.edu/blog/8-of-the-worlds-most-successful-people-with-adhd/
- University of Surrey. (2023, October). *New genes linked to ADHD identified potentially paving the way for new treatments.* https://www.surrey.ac.uk/news/new-genes-linked-adhd-identified-potentially-paving-way-new-treatments
- Upledger Institute International. "What Is CranioSacral Therapy?" *Upledger Institute International,* https://www.upledger.com/therapies/index.php. Accessed 16 June 2024.
- U.S. Department of Education. (n.d.). *A Guide to the Individualized Education Program. Retrieved from* https://www2.ed.gov/parents/needs/speced/iepguide/index.html
- U.S. Department of Education, Office for Civil Rights. (2016). *Know your rights: Students with ADHD. U.S. Department of Education.* https://www2.ed.gov/about/offices/list/ocr/docs/dcl-know-rights-201607-504.pdf
- WebMD. (n.d.). *ADHD diet and nutrition: Foods to eat & foods to avoid. WebMD.* https://www.webmd.com/add-adhd/adhd-diets
- WebMD. (n.d.). *8 tips for talking to your child about ADHD. WebMD.* https://www.webmd.com/add-adhd/childhood-adhd/features/adhd-talking-to-child
- WebMD. (n.d.). *Occupational therapy for children with ADHD. WebMD.* https://www.webmd.com/add-adhd/childhood-adhd/occupational-therapy-for-children-with-adhd
- Willingness. (n.d.). *How can I teach my kids emotional regulation? Willingness.* https://willingness.com.mt/how-can-i-teach-my-kids-emotional-regulation/
- Wrightslaw. (n.d.). *Special Education Advocacy. Retrieved from* https://www.wrightslaw.com/advoc/articles/advocacy_intro.htm
- Yale Medicine. (n.d.). *Self-care strategies for parents & caregivers. Yale Medicine.* https://medicine.yale.edu/news-article/self-care-strategies-parents/
- Zhang, Donna D., and Masaaki W. Itoh. "Nrf2: A Therapeutic Target for the

Prevention of Oxidative Stress Diseases." Antioxidants & Redox Signaling, vol. 11, no. 5, 2009, pp. 593-602.

www.ingramcontent.com/pod-product-compliance
Lightning Source LLC
Chambersburg PA
CBHW021623120626
46545CB00002B/374